Michael Finnigan

THEY DID YOU CAN

How to achieve whatever
~~YOU~~ ~~want~~ ~~in life~~ ~~with~~ the help
~~of~~ heroes

www.chpus.com

First published by

Crown House Publishing Ltd
Crown Buildings, Bancyfelin, Carmarthen, Wales, SA33 5ND, UK
www.crownhouse.co.uk

and

Crown House Publishing Company LLC
6 Trowbridge Drive, Suite 5, Bethel, CT 06801, USA
www.chpus.com

British Library of Cataloguing-in-Publication Data
A catalogue entry for this book is available
from the British Library.

13-digit ISBN 978-184590064-9

LCCN 2007922552

Edited by Fiona Spencer Thomas
Printed and bound in the UK by
The Cromwell Press, Trowbridge, Wiltshire

Acknowledgements

I owe so much to so many people but I do want to mention a few of them. First of all, Art Niemann, my mentor and inspiration. I never even would have got started on all this had it not been for his intervention in the early 1990s when my life was on pause. He taught me about the great W. Clement Stone and his positive life and business philosophies, and I am forever grateful. One day I promise I will write their stories.

My colleagues at Advance Performance have helped so much too, especially Gail Bailey who puts up with my considerable eccentricities with expertise, patience and humour, and Darcenia Teasdale, whose painstaking research has proved invaluable.

My family's pride in what I am striving to achieve keeps me going when the going is tough. Thanks Cheryl, my Wonder Woman; thanks Pauline, the Helicopter Flying Mum and Grandma; thanks David, Dad, Granddad and Fish Finger Butty Maker par excellence, and thanks Bob and Marie Wallbank, the in-laws of your dreams.

I am so determined to make them proud of me and to set a good example to my four gorgeous daughters, Lucy, Rose, Grace and Daisy. One thought of them and I can do anything.

My friends, some of whom are in the book, some of whom helped knock it into shape and some who just keep encouraging me, will probably never know how much they mean to me and I thank them all. No need to name them, they know who they are.

The people who gave up their time to appear in the pages have been inspirational and most generous. They have made the book worth doing and I hope that I have represented them all with the dignity and respect they deserve. I am humble and grateful.

My editor, Fiona Spencer Thomas, has really earned her fee on this project. I am sure I am her most difficult and demanding challenge but, no matter how awkward I have been, she has coped superbly and kept her calm in the face of it all. Her skill, coaching, friendship, long lunches and experience have been much appreciated.

Caroline Lenton, at Crown House, who is a bundle of energy, believed in the project from the very first moment we talked and gave it one hundred percent from then on. Without her, there would be no book. She has been an inexhaustible inspiration.

All these people are making my dream come true, proving, as the great Beth Tweddle says, that nothing is impossible.

Contents

Introduction

Let me tell you why I have written this book. Let me tell you about a time when I was a lot younger and in my final year at school and on track to get what I had always dreamed of, a contract to become an Apprentice Professional Footballer with Blackburn Rovers.

I had been 'spotted' when I was fourteen, and invited for a trial. I felt it was long overdue. I was an outstanding natural talent. A centre forward in the mould of Teddy Sheringham, Kenny Dalglish or Eric Cantona, not quick, but a great finisher and player of the killer two yard pass that splits defences. I averaged one goal and one assist per game and everyone knew I was going to make it. Everyone that is, except me.

The confidence I had when I was fourteen was going, fast. At Rovers, they picked you up on your faults and nobody reminded you how good you were, they just killed you when you made an error. I stopped enjoying it.

At school, John Allsopp and I (John was in my year and a terrific midfield player, just like Riise or the great David Beckham – he scored regularly with shots from our half!), left early every Tuesday and Thursday to train and even that became a chore. I would rather have stayed in Henshaw's History class than gone to play football. How bad is that?

A fear of failure slowly took hold of me. Instead of thinking 'won't it be great when…' I was thinking 'what if I don't make it?' or 'what if I'm not good enough?' I used to imagine the feelings of rejection and embarrassment so much that eventually they totally replaced the feelings of pride and excitement that I once had.

At the end of the season, I quit. I never told them. I just didn't go back and I never played football properly again, ever. I became a hero, in fact an anti-hero. "That's Finni; he could have been a footballer but he didn't want to," people would say. Wrong. "That's Finni; he could have been a footballer but he didn't have the bottle." That is what they should have been saying. That was the truth.

So what did I need? I needed inspiration. I needed to know that what I was feeling, everyone feels. I needed to be reminded that I was a fantastically gifted young man who took apart every defence he ever played against. I

Michael Finnigan

needed help with my focus and with my goals. It wasn't there, or if it was, I couldn't own up to anyone about how I was feeling anyway. Not even John Allsopp, who just went from strength to strength. Only a terrible knee injury stopped him, no human being ever could, certainly not himself! I needed my heroes to tell me that they felt just like I did. I know now that George Best did. He ran away from Manchester United the first time, all the way home to Belfast, but they brought him back. I know now, but I needed to know then.

This book was what I needed then; words of inspiration and advice from people who had been there and done it. I have written it so that you don't have to go through what I went through. I have written it so that you can reach your goal. I've written it so that you don't have to wait to discover the secrets of mental strength until you are thirty-two, like I did.

Let me tell you right now that you have enough talent to succeed in whatever you have set your heart on. Talent is never the real reason why people succeed. Too much talent is usually a curse. So don't go thinking you're not good enough. You are.

What will stop you is a loss of focus or self belief and this book will make sure that it cannot and does not happen.

Look, I can't do it all for you. You have to take these lessons from these great people and put them to use in your own life but *They Did You Can* will be there for you and so will the people who believe in you, to help you along the way.

Nothing great is achieved easily, nothing. Everyone struggles. Each one of us is fighting demons. We just have to beat them and our talent will then take care of the rest.

Share this book with your teachers, coaches, friends and your parents or guardians. Make sure that they know how to help you on your magnificent journey, whatever your dreams are.

You can make it. You will make it. Then you can appear in one of our future editions and inspire the next generation with a story or two of your own.

Come on!

Sir Tom Finney. Made 433 league appearances. Scored a club record of 187 goals.
Nicknamed 'The Preston Plumber.' after his part time job. Has 76 caps and scored 30 goals for England. Not bad for a plumber eh??

Foreword by Sir Tom Finney

Michael has asked me to write a few words and I suppose I had better explain who I am first.

I played seventy-six matches for England, mostly on the wing, a few as a centre forward, and was fortunate to score thirty goals which was a record for a while. I also played 433 games in what is now called the Premier League and scored 187 goals for my club, again mostly from the wing. We got to two FA Cup Finals, winning one and losing one, and were runners up in the League twice. Apparently I was also the first person to be voted Footballer of the Year twice. I played in three World Cups too.

Being a professional footballer was great and it was all I ever dreamed of as a child, the only thing I ever wanted to be when I grew up. However I must say that, although I was a good player as a boy, I not only had to battle a long glandular illness which meant going to hospital twice a week for many years, but I was also really tiny! Even when I was fourteen I weighed just five stone and was only four feet nine inches tall, and that was when I had my trial with Preston North End. They had said I was too small and wouldn't even let me have a trial, but my father met the Chairman in a bar and was so insistent that, eventually, they gave up and let me have a go! I owe a lot to my father.

I think my story proves that if you really want to do something you can do it, in spite of whatever problems you face.

I wasn't going to let anything get in the way of my dream and you shouldn't let anything get in the way of yours.

Sir Tom Finney

Foreword by Sir Clive Woodward

When Michael asked if I would write something for this book, I looked at the messages he was working on and thought how useful they would be to young people and to coaches too. So many of Michael's messages dovetail with my own philosophy which I encapsulated in my book *Winning*, which featured our success in bringing home the 2003 Rugby World Cup.

When thinking about individual or team sport, I look at people on three levels in an attempt to see where they are.

Participating is when your interest is to become actively involved for the enjoyment of taking part.

Competing means that you become serious about your sport to secure victories.

Winning is when you play at an elite level and become obsessed with being prepared to do whatever it takes to be victorious; where you have the drive and the motivation to excel and dominate in a competitive environment.

The great thing about this book is that it will help you, whatever your level of interest.

When I gave Jonny Wilkinson his England debut when he was only eighteen in what is a sport of immense physical contact, people said he wasn't ready, yet I knew that picking him was no gamble. There could be no doubt that Jonny wanted to be the very best, as his hours of kicking goals from the age of thirteen with coach Dave Alred proved.

If you enjoy what you do and work harder at it than anyone else, you will come to the attention of the right person at the right time and earn the 'lucky' break you deserve.

Jonny got the break that he deserved and, just a few years later, delivered that winning kick in the World Cup Final, as he had done in his mind a million times.

You need luck but you have to earn it (it is not a word that you will find in the index of my book!), and unless you love what you do and work hard, you'll be the one telling the 'hard luck' story.

However, if you put into action the ideas in this book, you will find that 'winning' is well within your reach.

Sir Clive Woodward

Foreword by David Moyes

As I write this, I have been manager of an English Premier League Football Club for several years, having previously managed a club in two lower divisions in England. Prior to this I was a professional footballer myself and made my debut for the mighty Celtic as a teenage centre half.

I suppose that, by now, I should have a pretty good idea of what it takes to 'make it' and play with distinction on a big stage. I have certainly seen plenty of people who should have made it and didn't for some reason; lots of people with talent, who fell by the wayside.

As I young player myself, I found it hard at times to cope with the demands of playing against top players in front of big crowds. I clearly remember being on the team coach on the way to a night match. I was sitting there feeling terrible when the floodlights came into view, shining brightly in the night. I remember looking at those lights and willing them to fail, hoping they would just blink out right before my eyes so that the game could be called off.

When you play at the highest level, it isn't because you don't have nerves before a game, it's because you learn how to deal with them and find a way to get through it all. You have to find your own way to deal with pressure; nobody else can tell you how to do it, because they are not you; you are unique, a one-off. Only you can find the answer.

Now fortunately, Michael, who has been working with us at Everton on exactly these kinds of things for a few years now, has written this book and interviewed people who have found the answer that you might be looking for. Their experiences will help you find your answer and so will Michael's ideas.

Michael and his colleagues at Advance have worked with some of the biggest names in sport and have proved time and again that they know exactly what it takes, mentally, to succeed.

What the book probably won't do, though, is give you the answer on a plate; life just isn't that simple or easy. You will have to work things out for yourself and, as a manager, that is one of the top things I look for in a player; the ability to think for yourself, to make decisions, to take control

David Moyes.
Football player.
Football manager.
Football mad!!!

of situations, to show initiative, to find a way to win. None of these is about your natural talent.

Success for me at the highest level in sport is about having the mental strength to make sure you play to one hundred percent of your potential, and Michael's book will help you to do that.

Read the chapters, learn the lessons, then find a way to put them into practice for yourself.

Good luck!

David Moyes

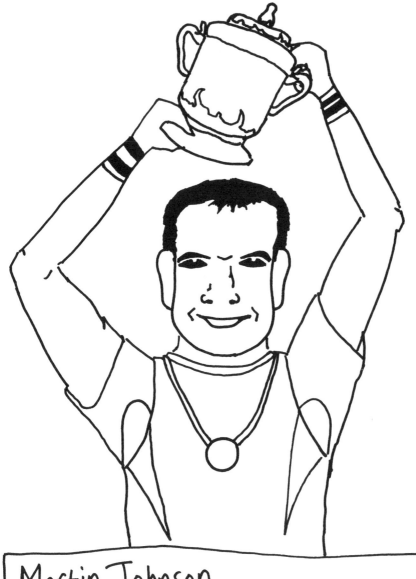

Martin Johnson.
Won the 2003 World Cup for England with team mate Jonny Wilkinson, or 'Wilko' as he calls him.

Foreword by Martin Johnson

People often ask me what sort of Churchillian speech I delivered at the end of full-time and prior to going out for extra time at the Rugby World Cup final back in 2003. They ask me how was I able to motivate a team of guys who had just had the trophy cruelly snatched away from them with just a few seconds to go of normal time.

Whilst I would love to go into great detail about how I rallied the guys and picked them up off the floor, to do so would be plain wrong. There were no big speeches, no brow beating and no rallying of the troops. And I guess this in a nutshell is one of the reasons why I agreed to write this foreword for Michael's book.

In his book Michael repeatedly talks about the importance of belief and focus and I think these are the words that would encapsulate that five-minute talk before starting extra time.

Just looking around the circle and into the eyes of the guys I instinctively knew at that point, we were going to win. They were a superb group of individuals, who had built up a huge sense of belief over the years through trust and confidence in each other. This sense of belief ensured we would be focused on what was needed to make sure the game was won.

Mike says in his book that talent alone is not enough and he is absolutely right. What that squad of guys had was a huge amount of talent coupled with a fierce belief and an unwavering commitment to focus on the job in hand. And that is why on that incredible night we were crowned World Champions.

Martin Johnson CBE

Chapter One

The Powerful Three

What is it that stands between you and having what you want? Is it 'luck'? Do you need a lucky break? Is success simply a matter of being in 'the right place at the right time' or is it a case of, 'it isn't what you know, it's who you know'?

Let me tell you right now that it is none of these. Success is not about getting lucky, and failure is not about being unlucky. It is all about you making the things happen that need to happen.

Have you heard the story about the world famous golfer Gary Player? As a young man he was preparing for a tournament by practising his bunker shots when a wise-cracking Texan challenged him to hole one of his next three shots. Player holed not one but two of the next three. Mr Wiseass said "that's just pure luck boy," and Player answered "Yeah, but you know sir, the harder I practise, the luckier I get."

In 1996 at Royal Lytham, I saw Jack Nicklaus do exactly the same thing from a hundred yards. So you see, the harder you practise, the luckier you do get!

That is the bottom line. No excuses.

The Bottom Line

Face it; nobody owes you a living.

What you achieve or fail to achieve in your lifetime is directly related to what you do, or fail to do.

People don't choose their parents or childhood, but you can choose your own direction.

> *Everyone has problems and obstacles to overcome but that too is relative to each individual.*
>
> *Nothing is carved in stone; you can change anything in your life if you want to badly enough.*
>
> *Excuses are for losers. Those who take responsibility for their actions are the real winners in life.*
>
> *Winners meet life's challenges head on, knowing there are no guarantees and give all they've got.*
>
> *Never think it's too early to begin. Time has no favourites and will pass whether you act or not.*
>
> *Take control of your life. Dare to dream and take risks ... Compete.*

The only thing that stands in your way is YOU; nothing else; absolutely nothing.

I promise you now that, if you listen to what the people in this book are saying to you and you take their ideas on board then work as hard as you possibly can, if you give absolutely one hundred percent of everything you have to give, then you will have your dream. You will make it happen and Fortune and Glory will be yours.

Let's take a look at **what** the three key psychological concepts are that you are going to master, before we start looking at **how** you are going to maximise your mental powers.

The Powerful Three are:

One The Tree of Greatness

Two The Creation of Beliefs

Three The Brain's Mighty Secret

1. The Tree of Greatness

Think of a tree for a minute. Break it down into five parts and what do you get? It's simple when you think about it. First you have the Leaves and/or the Fruit – apples, berries, chestnuts or whatever. Second you have the Branches. Third would be the Trunk. Fourth, below the ground, would come the Roots, then finally, the Soil surrounding it all.

Interestingly, in terms of motivation, human beings have the same five layers. Of course we're not covered in Leaves, but we do have five levels which we need to understand.

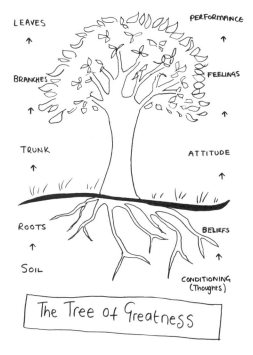

First, equivalent to Leaves, comes the way we Perform. That is what we want to learn about, isn't it? We want to learn how to be our best more often; how to win more often.

Write down words below that describe you when you perform at your very best.

The Tree of Greatness

Would you like to be like that more often? Of course you would, who wouldn't? **Let's commit to learning how to be on top form all the time!** Imagine how cool that would be.

Now, what are you like when you are at or close to being your worst? Write those words down. **This is known as being in 'The Zone'.**

```
_____

_____

_____

_____

_____
```

Sometimes that list is easier to write and we will find out why later; it's normal, so relax!

Let's commit now to being more aware of when we are like this and seeing it as a signal to refocus. You're going to learn how to do it later and, in fact, you are going to become so good at recognising this and changing it, that it is going to become easy.

Now, let's go to the second level, the **Branches**. These are your **Feelings**. Write down how you feel when you are performing really well.

```
_____

_____

_____

_____

_____
```

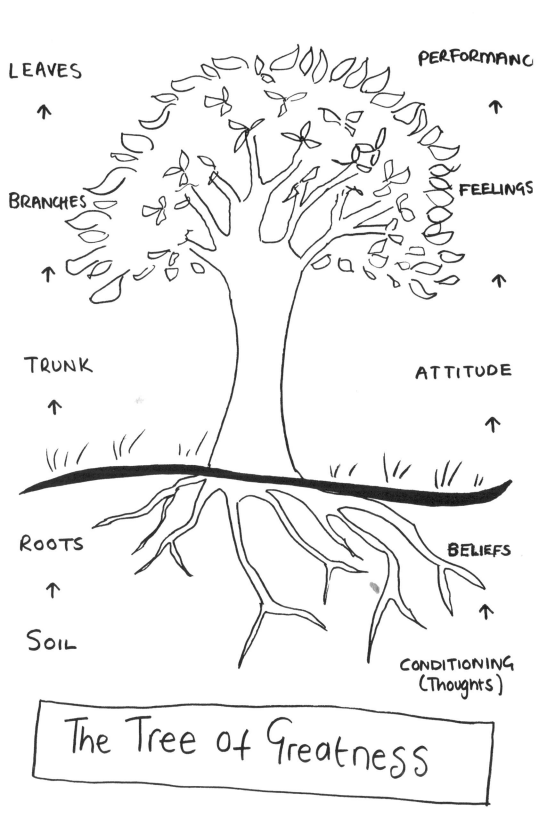

LEAVES

PERFORMANC

BRANCHES

FEELINGS

TRUNK

ATTITUDE

ROOTS

BELIEFS

SOIL

CONDITIONING
(Thoughts)

The Tree of Greatness

Now you can start to connect good feelings to good performance. Feeling awful and performing well do not go together at all. Again, let's be more aware of this so we can change it.

Recognising that you are not in 'The Zone' is the biggest step you have to take to get back in there!

Equally, let's recognise when we are in The Zone, so that we get used to what it's like, then we can more easily re-create it.

The third level of a tree is the **Trunk** which, in human terms, is our **Attitude**.

This means our Attitude to everything. It is our Attitude towards things that makes us feel a certain way and those Feelings will dictate our Performance.

That is why our Attitude is so important. Look at what South African cricketer, Eric Simons has to say about attitude in Chapter 3. This means not letting things get us down or put us off. It means not making excuses but instead, accepting responsibility for where we are or what we have done when things don't go our way; not putting our heads in the sand, pretending things are fine when they are not.

Losers think that when something goes wrong, it is ninety percent related to a thing that has happened which is beyond their control, and only ten percent down to their Attitude. The Losers will blame anything and anyone before looking at themselves. They spend all their time and energy looking for excuses and scapegoats. You will hear them saying things like:

'It wasn't my fault'

'It was the referee'

'It was my shoes'

'It was the bad weather'

'It's my hopeless teacher'

'We hit the post'

'We didn't have enough money'

'I didn't get a chance to show what I can do'

'We live in a rough area'

Any old excuse will do!

If you find yourself competing against people who say things like that, you are going to beat them! They have lost already.

However, Winners think that, when something goes wrong, it is only ten percent related to something which has happened, and ninety percent down to their Attitude. Winners accept responsibility, and believe that they have the power to sort it out. Winners spend their time thinking how to get things right, whilst the Losers are still busy looking for their alibis!

Let's commit now to NEVER letting anyone or anything get us down!

Your Attitude will determine the way you feel and that, in turn, will deliver the Performance – good or bad. YOU decide!

Now, the **Roots** of the tree are equivalent to our **Beliefs**. So, what do you truly believe about the future and what it has in store for you? Do you really believe you are good enough to have what it is that you want? Do you really, deep down inside, believe that you deserve success and happiness? Or do you believe that your goals are only wishes, and hopes, destined never to be realised?

Google Cliff Young for me, right now.

You will find that this guy ran 875 kilometres in less than seven and a half days. Everyone thought you ran this long-distance race by averaging 125 kilometres each day, sleeping in a van driven by your team mates, then running the same distance the next day. Running 125 kilometres a day is roughly like running three marathons. However, Cliff was a farmer and he was entering this type of race for the first time. Nobody told him you needed a van and nobody told him you were supposed to sleep! He just didn't know. So guess what he did? Well, just like good old Forrest Gump in the movie – he ran! He ran all day, every day, stopping every so often for cat naps. He ran the whole way, not in seven and a half days but in FIVE days, fifteen hours, and four minutes – TWO days faster than anyone else!

Now, what did Cliff's PERFORMANCE do to the BELIEFS of the other runners, not for the same race, but the year after? Do you think they all brought vans? Of course not. Remember, they had never run the distance without sleeping. They had only seen someone else do it and so changed what they believed was possible. Of course, the next year hardly anyone slept and running the race in five days became the norm.

When you change what you BELIEVE, you can change the way you PERFORM.

By the way, when Cliff Young ran that race, he was sixty-one years old! What about that!

Finally, we come to the **Soil** or, in human terms, our **Conditioning**. Who conditions us as we grow?

Parents?	*yes*
Brothers and sisters?	*yes*
Teachers?	*yes*
People on television?	*yes*

And many others besides.

> **One guy in America, a Dr Helmstetter, reckons that in the first sixteen years of our lives, people say 'No' to us 148,000 times. Get out a calculator and divide 148,000 by 16 and then by 365; it comes to 25.**

Twenty-five times each and every day in those first sixteen years, someone will tell us 'No'. This makes us get used to listening to others and taking on board what they believe. In the same sixteen years, on average, people will sit us down and tell us how great we are only three or four times, so the vast majority of the conditioning we get is negative, not positive. The result is that it is keeping us away from danger and getting us used to being wrong, or having our suggestions ridiculed, or just making us feel unimportant; less important than the grown-up watching a television programme or sitting in a chair.

'No! Keep away from that fire!'
'No! You can't read your book! Go to sleep!'
'No, I'm too tired to play football with you.'

We hear 'No' a lot more than we hear 'Yes', so much so that we get used to being wrong, fearing things we don't understand and, as a result, we stop taking risks. How many times when the teacher asked a question, did you know the answer but failed to raise your hand?

Of all the factors and people that condition us, by far the most powerful is ourselves. Why? Because, conditioning is only the way we **THINK**; and thinking is ninety percent attitude and only ten percent fact. If someone thinks you won't be able to do something, their opinion counts for nothing unless it becomes yours.

We have to learn to stand up for ourselves; to stop ourselves thinking negative thoughts, because they build negative beliefs and negative attitudes, they breed negative feelings and they lead to negative performances!

> **Let's commit right now to not allowing anyone else to tell us who we are going to be, or what we are going to achieve! Let's commit to deciding for ourselves.**

> *'I don't have to be what you want me to be; I'm free to be what I want'*
>
> Muhammad Ali

Ultimately then, what we are saying is that thinking is the key to success because, by learning to control our thoughts, we automatically control our performance.

We call this Miracle Grow for human beings, and this is what we are going to learn to master.

2. The Creation of Beliefs

Let me ask you a few questions which might seem unrelated, but which are actually all pointing to essential information which we need right now. I want you to really think about them, then I will explain my point, and will finally answer them for you later. Okay? Great! Here goes.

How do our minds process information?

How do we remember things so well when they happened so long ago?

Why do we get hungry when somebody mentions food?

Why is it that the very mention of 'freshly cut grass', makes us think we can smell it?

(For me, you only have to say the word 'whisky' and I feel instantly sick! I can smell it now, it's horrific, and there isn't a bottle within a hundred yards of me!)

Why can my daughters not hold cotton wool and why do they cringe and hide their eyes when their baby sister bites a clean towel?

Why do some people look away from a snake on the television?

Why did my daughter lift her feet off the floor when she was watching that scene with the rats from *Indiana Jones and the Last Crusade*?

Why is this relevant? Let me explain.

When your brain observes something in the world outside your head, it remembers the picture it is seeing by translating it into a description, using Words. Those Words describe the Picture as you see it (not necessarily as it really is) and the Picture, if it is a special one, is filled with Emotion.

Words → Pictures → Emotions

'A picture paints a thousand words'

Think about the saddest or funniest moments in your life. The saddest, if you experienced them deeply and stored them properly in your mind, will come back to you very strongly; the pictures will be as clear as if the event happened yesterday and you may find yourself 'welling up' inside, maybe even fighting back a tear.

If I just think, for a few seconds, of my brother, who died of cancer a few years ago, I can feel the tears coming, even today. If I think about the funniest moments from *Only Fools and Horses*, where they are standing underneath the wrong chandelier, or where Del goes to lean coolly on the bar and misses it, or when The Simpsons are giving each other so many electric shocks that all the lights go out in Springfield, or the time in *Friends* where Joey appears at the door with his head inside the turkey, I instantly start to smile, maybe even laugh and I'm probably nowhere near a television!

When you get together with mates, you will usually start talking about times when something funny happened to you and, within seconds, you will all be laughing your heads off.

**Remember this: Memories powerfully stored
will be powerfully recalled.**

And what about this? What is your equivalent of the whisky thing, or snakes, or spiders, or cotton wool, or towelling? Whatever it is, I guarantee that you cringe, not just when you experience that thing, but even when you just THINK about it or when someone mentions it in conversation. My wife just cannot handle the word 'runny'; it makes her feel sick. How weird is that? I cannot look at an action replay that shows a footballer breaking a leg, I just can't! Why?

Imagine if you only flinched when these things were really happening to you. Now, if it's a harmless spider walking by or someone offering you a whisky, then big deal. But let's change the spider to a tiger. If you were walking in a jungle and thought you saw a tiger fifty yards away, what would you do? Would you say to yourself, 'ignore it, it was probably just the sun on some leaves,' or would you say to yourself, 'is that a tiger? Better get out of here quick!' Within seconds, your heart would be pumping, your adrenalin levels would be high, your breathing would be shallow and you would be running as fast as you could!

You would not be hanging around, saying to yourself, 'I'll just go over and have a look; no sense getting all sweaty if it was just a trick of the light!' Live like that and you would be dead in no time – Tiger Fast Food!

Our brains are trained to react to things as if they are real, even when they turn out not to be.

Try this on someone you know who blushes. Ask them what makes them blush and, within seconds of you asking the question – when they are thinking about embarrassing events in their life – watch them blush before your very eyes!

The killer point here, is that:

The brain does not know the difference between a real and imagined experience!

The brain responds to events which it thinks are real, whether they are or not. This is why we cringe at the snakes, the whisky, the cotton wool, the towels or even the word 'runny' in my wife's case. It also explains why people say they are afraid of or dislike things they have never experienced. Over the years I have heard people say things like: 'I am terrified of flying' or 'I don't like prawns' only to find out that they have never been on a plane or have never tasted prawns. So what they mean is that they don't like the THOUGHT of flying or of eating prawns, and that's different, isn't it?

Try this; when I get together with my kids, two of whom are grown up now and two still small, occasionally I will say, "I'm going to count to ten and then we're going to start laughing." At ten, I start to laugh and they just can't help it. Within minutes, we are in bits, begging each other to stop laughing! They are laughing at the THOUGHT of laughing.

One of my business partners used to tell his son, Tom, that he could see that his nose was itchy; in seconds, Tom would scratch his nose!

Have you noticed your reaction when someone yawns? Try that one at the next family party; just yawn at someone and then watch them. They will yawn within seconds because YOU made THEM THINK about YAWN-ING. Works every time!

This vital principle forms the basis of one of the secrets of the champions, the art of 'visualisation', which we will come on to later.

Did you get the answers to the questions I asked earlier? Of course you did. Our brains make us act on things whether they are real or only imagined, and whether they make sense or not. This great secret forms the basis of visualisation, as you will hear from Amanda Kirby later.

By the way, I never tortured my kids with cotton wool, they just don't like it! When I was eighteen and discovered whisky, however, I really did drink too much of it one night and have never touched a drop since! Sometimes our actions are based on logic and on experience, but not always!

3. The Brain's Mighty Secret

Ben Carson had a tough childhood in America. His father left home, his mother was in and out of work and he and his brother were always in trouble at school. Because they were a 'welfare family', they were constantly moved from one town to another.

Ben's school work was poor and he decided that, if he was going to be thrown out of school, he didn't want to be labelled 'stupid', so when he did so badly in maths that he became embarrassed, he threw over a desk and so got himself thrown out with what he thought was the better label of being 'aggressive' instead! When this worked, it became a habit; whenever classes got hard, he would go crazy and get thrown out again.

Eventually his mother got sick of this and told him and his brother that there was to be no more television until reading and homework were done and even then, only a little. She worked them hard and marked everything they did, praising them for their good work.

Ben started to do better in school and showed that he was actually pretty bright. One day he asked his mother to help him with some school work. "Ben," she told him, "I can't read." He was amazed. All that time, his mother had been setting him work, marking it, and praising him for how good it was and how clever he was proving he could be, and all the time she was faking it!

Remember what we just learned, though.

The brain does not know the difference between a real and imagined experience.

Ben's mother caused him to start thinking and then believing, 'Hey, I'm smart actually!' Once he started to believe it, he started to perform after year upon year of failure and misery.

> **'I am the greatest'; I said that even before I knew I was. I figured that if I said it enough, I would convince the world that I really was the greatest**
>
> Muhammad Ali

By the way, that little black boy, Ben Carson, now works at Johns Hopkins Hospital in Baltimore, Maryland, and grew up to be the world's leading paediatric neurosurgeon.

Ben works with children who suffer from a rare form of epilepsy. He pioneered a surgical procedure called a hemispherectomy, and found that children who had the operation not only made full recoveries but started to pick up things that they had lost the ability to do before the operation, like Matthew, who had been unable to continue with his violin lessons but played again with no problem after the operation. Doesn't Ben's experience just prove that you can achieve whatever you want? There he was, a young guy failing at school and now, he's a pioneering surgeon!

Ben explains that the brain's cells, or neurons to give them their proper name, connect when we decide to do something, like hit a tennis ball for example. We have around ten billion neurons and hitting a tennis ball only occupies a few of them. However, once those neurons involved in hitting the ball have come together to hit the ball, they stay literally linked by the chemical reaction that goes on between them. The links between the neurons, formed by the electro-chemical reaction, are called **dendrites**.

Once you form a set of dendrites in your brain to hit a tennis ball, that same set of dendrites is activated by the chemical reaction every time you hit the ball, and each time those dendrites get wider. Eventually they form what Carson calls 'pathways' in the brain, going from small ones to roads, to dual carriageways and, eventually, to motorways and super highways, capable of allowing the chemical to travel really quickly.

This, of course, means that your reactions improve; you can see the ball earlier, even when it is coming towards you quickly, and return it effortlessly.

One of the qualities of the sporting greats is that they always seem to have so much time to do things. I can tell you from fielding in the slips in practise with the South African Cricket Team, that when a batsman edged a ball bowled by my friend Makaya Ntini, captain Graeme Smith caught the ball when I was standing right next to him and hadn't moved. I hadn't even seen it! Graeme's dendrites for catching a cricket ball were much wider than mine. Why? Because he practised so often and every time he caught a ball, he used the same dendrites and, each time, the chemical made them wider so he could catch a ball flying at incredible speeds.

Practice really does make perfect!

Now, try this. Find a ball or an apple, something round and not too heavy, that you can throw. Throw it to someone, just a few feet away and ask them to throw it back to you. Do it again, a little faster this time. Do this a few times. Now, go to throw the ball, but hold on to it, just making them think you are going to throw it.

Write what happens:

```



.......................................................................................................

.......................................................................................................

.......................................................................................................

.......................................................................................................

.......................................................................................................

.......................................................................................................

.......................................................................................................


```

Yes, they moved their hands, didn't they? They went to catch it even though you kept hold of it. Why?

The brain does not know the difference between a real and imagined experience!

The dendrites said to their brain 'come on, move those hands, the ball is coming!' and the brain responded. It has to, it has no choice.

Now, for the hands to move, the muscles have to move and for the muscles to move, the brain has to send a signal and the signal is sent by chemicals via the neurons and dendrites.

Now think about this. Remember that every time the chemical moves, the dendrite gets wider, making the journey easier for the chemical next time. So dendrites get wider, not when we **DO** things, but when we **THINK** about doing things. **Thinking** starts the chain that leads to **Performance**. Remember this from earlier? The Tree?

Now, if we have a fault or a bad habit, this is bad news. It means that every time we think about that thing, we make it worse because we make the dendrite wider.

Think about it this way. If you take a single twig from a bush, two feet long, and try to snap it, you will do it easily. Imagine that as being a thin, little dendrite. Now take fifty twigs and bundle them together; not only can you not snap them, they could support your whole weight! Dendrites are exactly the same.

I was playing with an elastic band the other day and I started wondering how far I could throw it. The answer was not far, so then I flicked it and it went quite a bit further; then I tied it in a few knots and threw it and it went a bit further. I concluded that one elastic band, acting alone, was not terribly impressive but then I found an old elastic band ball I had been building for weeks; it was bigger than a golf ball. I went to the park outside our office, and threw this thing miles. Together the bands were powerful, just like strong dendrites are, but alone, one band or one thought, was not enough to achieve anything significant.

So how long does it take to turn a harmless elastic band into a powerful rubber ball, or how long does it take to replace an old negative dendrite with a powerful new one? Well that depends on how much work you apply to this simple formula:

I x F
Intensity x Frequency

Building a dendrite is simply a question of Intensity (how much emotion and power you place behind each thought that you have, either a little or a lot), and Frequency (how often you consciously work on that new thought). It really is that simple. Let's start work on some new positive dendrites right now:

'Repetition is the mother of skill'

Old Egyptian Proverb

(Egyptian schools were known as 'halls of repetition')

Write down the things you are no good

> I am no good at ....
>
> ....
>
> I am hopeless at ....
>
> ....
>
> I ....
>
> ....
>
> I ....
>
> ....

But here is the good news. If you can make a new, good dendrite and make that bigger than the old, bad one, your performance will change.

It really is as simple as that. And we are going to show you how to do it; no tricks, no embarrassment and no side effects, apart from excessive levels of success.

Now write down all the new dendrites we are going to build together:

> I am now great at ....
>
> ....
>
> I ....
>
> ....
>
> I ....
>
> ....
>
> I ....
>
> ....

I will show you how to build on this later.

So there you have the three powerful concepts we are going to use as the basis for our learning together. We will refer back to them many times during the book, so keep them clear in your mind.

Chapter Two

The Best Friend

Having a best friend is one of the greatest things in the world. Someone you can share with, laugh with, do things with. When things are bad, they are the ones who can support you and help you get through. Have you ever considered who might be your best friend? Did you ever realise that it is, in fact, you? Or at least it should be. Who knows what you need? Who knows what your innermost thoughts are and who knows the words you need to hear for encouragement? Well that's the way it should be but that same best friend is often your worst enemy. The one that sabotages everything you try to do. The one that says 'you'll fail' or 'you're useless'.

I talked to my friend Philip Neville about how he made it to the top and where he got his encouragement from.

Philip joined Everton and immediately gave everyone a huge lift. It took him no time at all to win over the Chairman, Bill Kenwright, who said "Philip Neville? The easiest person I ever dealt with. He made it very clear to me that he wanted to play for us and so the contractual terms were very easy to agree."

Words like 'committed' and 'professional' could have been written just for him. He is a bundle of energy and as passionate about football and winning as any person you could ever meet.

He also just happens to be one of the most successful English footballers of all time. Very few people win the FA Cup (three times), let alone the Premier League (six times), or the Champions League, or the World Club Championship and never all four in the same year. Philip has won eleven major trophies so far in a distinguished career. He was a member of that all-conquering team of 1999, and has played for his country fifty-two times, many of those with his brother, Gary, which is another rare achievement.

I was desperate to find out what had made that team so special.
'Complete dedication and sacrifice from every single person. When you want to be a successful team, you have all got to be in it, not just two or

Philip Neville has won the FA Cup 3 times, the Premier League 6 times, the Champions League and the World Club Championship. He once won all four in one year.

He has won 11 trophies, played for his country 52 times, many with his brother Gary.

That sounds like a pretty successful career when you add it all up! (And he's still going!!)

three, or some going in different directions, but all of you pulling in the same direction, even your families. The sacrifices are immense.'

How does that start? How does it build? *'We had a turning point in that season. In our Champions League Group, we faced Juventus who we had never beaten and who we looked up to, if I'm honest. They had the likes of Alessandro Del Piero, and Zinedine Zidane, both great players. We beat them 3-2 on the night, and we came off having given everything we had. The next morning the manager got us all together and told us that, to win the Champions League, you had to come off at the end of every game exactly like that.*

Every time we played in Europe after that, he always brought us back to that game saying "Remember what it takes to win a game in Europe," and that was always at the back of our minds, so it was a turning point. We had given everything but actually won, so we knew we could do it again. He told us that if we did that again and again and again, then we would win the European Cup. He did it again in the Final when we came off at half-time losing 1-0. He reminded us then. In fact, what he was doing was making each member of the team believe in himself.'

Philip's football adventure really began at the age of eleven when he joined Manchester United. Excellence and the expectation that you would win things were hammered into him right from the start. *'I remember a practice game between the local lads and the lads from out of town, taken by Brian Kidd who, at the time, was the Youth Development Officer. I was centre back, and I just used to clear the ball up-field as far as I could, like you did in the Sunday League but Brian Kidd said "Phil, no. Play with the ball, pass it." Even then I remember thinking that I had to do better. Brian wasn't worried about you making mistakes, he just wanted you to play and wanted you to try things.*

I remember thinking I would have to raise the bar not only every time I played but every time I trained; I would have to show that I was improving, every single time. Each time you went into the Cliff Training Ground, you knew that Nobby Stiles and Brian Kidd, who had both won the European Cup when they were players and who you looked up to, were going to push you. They would make you play under real pressure every time to see if you could cope with it. You knew you had to get better every time and a lot of people just could not live with that pressure to produce every single time, not technically, just mentally,. If you can't hack it on a Tuesday night at a training ground, how on earth are you going to cope in front of 60,000 people?'

Did Philip know he was going to make it through the fire at any stage? *'I never ever thought I would play for the first team until I made my debut in the Derby game. I always thought I was a million miles away.'*

That's quite a revelation for a person who went on to achieve so much. *'I used to look at all the legends who had played for the club, and looked at the manager, and even at the players around me in the Youth Team like Beckham, Giggs and Scholes, and just thought they were all so far up there compared to me.'*

What was it like to be told he was making his debut? *'The team was just read out and I was in it. There was no fuss. I was eighteen. It was surreal. There was no big deal made about it, you were just expected to get on with it. It was a dream come true. Looking back now, I realise that if you have that innocence of youth, that excitement, that passion, I just don't think you can fail.*

When you get your chance, you just have to take it at United. If you see players play the odd game, then go back to the Reserves, they won't make it. They only pick you if they think you're ready, so if you don't make it, then that's it. When they pick you, you have to do well and stay in.'

Doesn't that sound brutal! Well it is! He really made me laugh when he told me about the day when he really felt at home, like he had made it as a footballer. *'All we ever aimed for was to get a Club Car, which you got after twenty appearances and five of us got one all together, Butty, Scholesy, Giggs, Becks and me. There were these five brand new Honda Preludes outside and that was it, we knew then we had made it! That was what all the lads used to aim for!'* (A Honda Prelude? Are you sure?)

So what was special about him amongst all those other kids who dreamed the dream? *'I put my success down to dedication, that's all. It isn't talent and if you want to prove that, then just look at my brother. He couldn't even get in his county side, he was just a town team player but he just had this vision that he was going to play for Man United; he wasn't bothered about anything else, so not getting into the county team didn't deter him at all.*

When he went to Man United with all these brilliant young players, he grew as he was determined to show them all he could do it. You have to have determination, sacrifice and dedication, and if you have talent as well, like say, Beckham or Giggs, then you are going to be a superstar. But if you're just like me and my brother, then just sheer hard work and dedication can get you through if you want it badly enough. There were loads

"... We knew we had made it!"
- Philip Neville.

of lads with more talent than me and my brother, but they didn't want it. They wanted to go out on a Saturday night, or stay with their friends from school, but we didn't!'

The Neville family is really unusual. Philip and his brother are both footballers and his sister has played netball for England too. *'My Mum and Dad were sports mad, so we all played and watched everything, football, cricket, rounders, netball. We were so close we all used to go to everything together, everything.'*

I was interested to see if this mental giant had ever got it wrong at any point. *'Oh yeah! My one big regret is around the World Cup in 1998. Glenn Hoddle was the Manager, and for three months before and six months afterwards, for the only time in my life, the whole experience got the better of me. Leading up to it, I put too much emphasis on it, and afterwards, when I didn't get selected, it was a massive downer.'*

He looks back on it now as the best thing that ever happened to him. *'It toughened me up and gave me a kick up the backside. It affected me so much that I was playing poorly. If you're playing poorly you're not in the team and if you're not in the team, then you're going to get replaced, sold.'*

That is an awful long time for a person to allow something to get to them but people do, we're human, even Philip Neville, but how did he get out of it? *'I just took a look at myself and didn't like what I was doing. I was bitter towards the England manager, when I should have been looking at myself and realising that I wasn't playing well enough to get in. I was blaming other people, when I should have been looking at myself, saying, "Right, I didn't get in, move on," and that is exactly what I did in 2002; I didn't get in and the following season I had my best ever season, so I learned from it.*

The first time he missed selection it took nine months out of his life, but the second time? *'It didn't even affect me, not one bit.* **Something good always comes out of something bad.** *It was just another learning experience that life throws you all the time.'*

Who were the people he had seen with the most mental strength? *David Beckham, without a doubt. You look at what he has had to cope with, yet he just goes out there and performs and, in his time, he has been truly world class. Abuse, death threats, tabloid lies, people following him everywhere, kidnap plots on his children, you name it and all through it he has won everything.*

There's also Roy Keane, of course. In the semi-final against Juventus we were 3-1 down on aggregate, 2-0 on the night, and he scored a great header just before half-time to get us back in the game. He didn't even celebrate, he just turned and ran back to our half and said "let's go again", and his eyes, his eyes ... he was just in the zone, he lived in the zone! You only saw the best of him when the chips were down. If things were all on an even keel, you never noticed him but when it mattered, he grew and you could see the other team just caving in.'

We often talk about how many people like that you can have in a team. Philip had a strong view. *'You need at least five or six who are unbreakable and in 1999 we had about ten and that's why it was so special. We had people on our bench who were mentally stronger than people in the opposition starting eleven! That is powerful. It creates an aura in the dressing room that intimidates the other team when you're face to face. The Manager used to say that you know when you are a good team when you look round the room before you go out and say "I wouldn't swap any of you for anyone else."'*

Why did he think Sir Alex Ferguson has been so successful? *'His work ethic is unbelievable and that rubs off on everyone else. He's hard, fair, and I will always take that, because nothing he ever did or said was personal, it was to make you better or the club better. He only had one goal, and that was to make Man United great, so if that meant upsetting a few people, so be it. The players he fell out with were those who thought it was personal and couldn't take it for what it was. As you get older and he trusts you, you realise he likes you and that he is a nice guy.*

When we lost on a Saturday, we got the biggest rollicking of our lives but on Sunday morning it was all forgotten. It was the same when we won too. For me that is a sign of class. He might think you have cost him dearly the day before but he moves on, because he still believes in you, because if he didn't believe in you, you wouldn't be there! Some people would avoid him, but they couldn't take it.'

Even more impressive for me though was what Philip told me about what happened when the team won. *'He enjoys it for thirty seconds, even a Cup Final, then he starts thinking about the next challenge. He treats winning and losing the same and says put it behind you, quickly.'*

I asked what Philip would say to a young person starting out. *'Go for it, no half measures, give it one hundred percent, be unbelievably dedicated and make sacrifices but make sure you're enjoying it. Whatever you do in life, only do it if you enjoy it.'*

Coach Says

1. Meet with triumph and disaster and treat these two impostors just the same.
2. Don't blame others when it goes wrong; look at yourself, accept responsibility.
3. Work to become 'unbreakable'.

Now write down what You Say below. To help you get started, you might say something like 'The next time I play badly I will take responsibility for it rather than blaming the others in my team.'

1. ....
....
2. ....
....
3. ....
....

Wouldn't it be great to have your best friend with you when you need them most? **Look at where Philip talks about not blaming others and looking at yourself**. He had to talk to himself as a best friend to break out of his 'downer'.

Why is that? Well, here's my opinion. If I think of my best friend, what that person brings to me is **honesty**, **encouragement**, **support** and **acceptance**; whether you succeed or fail, they will still be there for you.

Let's look a little deeper.

Honesty

Your best friend will tell you what you **need** to hear, as opposed to **what** you want to hear. When you do hear it, you know it is meant to help you and that their words carry no ill meaning of any kind. When you are getting too big for your boots, they will tell you. When you are embarrassing yourself, they will tell you. When you're being too hard on yourself, they will tell you. When they think you are showing complacency, they will give you a reality check, and when you doubt yourself or are feeling scared, they will remind you how brilliant you are.

Encouragement

Your best friend can tell when those negative thoughts have crept in; when you are using those old negative dendrites, instead of the positive ones. They can just tell because they know you so well, like I could when I was working with Jimmy White and Darren Clarke.

When your best friend senses fear or self-doubt in you, they are right there with words that remind you how great you are, unbeatable, invincible, the greatest. Imagine that friend was Muhammad Ali; he would have poems about you and lines to make you stand tall and bellow with laughter to lighten you up.

Most people don't know that Ali himself had a guy called Bundini Brown who he kept close to him. People would see Brown and wonder what he did as they never saw him working, but Ali kept him close because Brown would remind Ali how great he was. Brown is thought to have made up a lot of the lines Ali took credit for, like

"Float like a Butterfly, Sting like a Bee"

Your best friend knows when you need a boost to your morale and is there to provide that boost.

Support

Your best friend will do anything for you, give you whatever you need because, in their mind, 'what they have is yours'. They will defend you when others attack you, whether you are there or not. They will always believe the best of you.

Support is something you need when you're hurting, when you've failed or been defeated, and it is then that they will be there to listen and keep you on an even keel.

Acceptance

Win or lose, you are still their friend. They won't judge you or fade in and out of your life depending on how well you're doing. They are there for you; full stop.

As long as, deep down, you stay true to your values, they will be there for you and they won't be sitting in judgement over you.

So ...

Whose best friend are you? You must be somebody's. Why is that? Do you know? Have you asked them? Well, do it; find out what it is they like about you, and why they have chosen you when they could have chosen someone else. Write down why you think it is.

But, somebody else needs you as a best friend and, the thing is, you already are their friend, just not a very nice one! When you speak to the person I'm talking about, you don't always follow the four principles of honesty, encouragement, support and acceptance, and that's a shame because this person really needs you. Nobody else will do. In fact, if you talked to your other friends the way you talk to this one, you would lose them all! So who is this friend who needs you so much?

Look in a mirror, any mirror, and you'll find him or her staring right back at you, because it's **you**!

You

You must learn, very quickly, to become your **own** Best Friend. You are the one who is always there when you are needed. You are the one who always knows exactly when a word is required. You are the one who knows exactly what to say. Think about the times when you've needed someone to tell you something positive and you've known the exact words you wanted to hear.

Let me show you how to do this – properly; in fact so well, that you will never have to rely on words of encouragement from other people ever again!

What you say to yourself will determine what you believe about yourself; what you believe about yourself determines how you will perform.

Say → Believe → Perform

Let's do an example. Think of something about yourself that you currently do but would like to improve. Write down what it is; describe what happens whenever you try to do this thing. For example, if you wanted to be able to stand up in front of your class and say something, what happens at the moment? Do you put your hand up, then put it back down? Do you stand up and start going 'errrr'? Put down how you perform in the box below.

Perform: ....
....
....
....
....

Good. Now, describe what you believe about yourself in relation to this thing, whatever it is.

Believe: ....
....
....
....
....

Fine. Now, write down the thoughts that run through your mind and the words that come out of your mouth, every time you either think about it or talk about it to a friend.

Say: ....

....

....

....

....

Now, look back at them, following our formula:

Say → Believe → Perform

This means that whenever you think about this or it comes up in conversation, you say this, believe this so perform like this.

When you look at what you have written you will realise that it is no wonder you are unhappy with the way you perform. You will also realise that you are not helping yourself by saying those things because you are building negative beliefs (negative dendrites). So

**WYSIWYG
(What You Say Is What You Get)**

So you really need to turn this around and I will show you how. Look at this example about working out and notice the difference in the two performances because of the change in beliefs.

<table>
<tr><td>

(Old) Worst Enemy

I make excuses and go weeks without doing anything

I am unfit and too busy to change things

I'll give it a miss tonight I can't be bothered tonight It's boring

</td><td>

(New) Best Friend

I work out every other day, and love it!

I am fitter than I have ever been, have loads of energy and feel good

I love working out. I can't wait to get out there. I feel fantastic!

</td></tr>
</table>

How do we change this?

Go forward in time. Imagine, if you can, a time when whatever is happening now is no longer happening. This might be a month from now, three months, or even twelve. It really doesn't matter; just find in your mind a picture of a time when this negative thing isn't happening to you any more. Now, write down what that picture looks like and how it makes you feel.

Perform: .... Time:.................. (months)

....

....

....

....

Great, what a difference!

Now you need to describe what you are going to have to believe about yourself to make this happen.

Believe: ....
....
....
....
....

Excellent! Now, what new things are you going to say to yourself to change what you believe whenever this crops up in conversation or whenever you think about it.

Say: ....
....
....
....
....

Just look back up the page now at how different the two sets of statements are – chalk and cheese! No wonder you were having a problem.

Now all you have to do is, do it. Next time this crops up, say the new thing, not the old thing. It will take time but I promise you this works.

Just look how different those two columns on the previous page are. The point is that, when you change what you say, you change what you believe and, when you change what you believe, you change how you perform.

Change your thinking and you change your destiny!

You might think 'it can't be that easy' but it is.

They Did You Can

Using your 'Best Friend', is one of the most powerful techniques for change I have ever come across. Use it, always. The effects are astonishing and often immediate.

> *'I am The Greatest'*
>
> Muhammad Ali

Chapter Three

The Snap Out

We all have times when everything seems to go wrong and the world seems to be conspiring to make us fail or lose. 'It's not my fault,' we think, 'I'm just unlucky, or jinxed.' **Well that's just not the case because it's all about attitude**. You may be lucky to have the breaks but it's what you do with them that makes the difference between success and failure.

One of the best examples of this I have ever come across is Gordon Banks. Basically, this man is the greatest goalkeeper that ever lived, bar absolutely none.

He won the World Cup in 1966, never even conceding a goal until the semi-final and that was a penalty. He made the greatest save ever in the 1970 World Cup in Mexico from Pelé. He won the League Cup twice as a player and was Footballer of the Year in 1972.

Irish author, Don Mullan, wrote *Gordon Banks: A Hero Who Could Fly*, which is to form the basis of a feature film. Mullan, a young boy growing up during the troubles in Northern Ireland, claims that Banks prevented him from joining the IRA. "I was his greatest save," says Don Mullan.

Now that is a Hero. And let me tell you how it feels to talk to a Hero (because I did).

My legs feel as if they are made of lead, my hands are shaking; I can hear the nerves in my voice. I have just come off the phone to Gordon Banks. Yes, Gordon Banks, The Gordon Banks. Why am I like this? I have spoken to loads of people like Gordon but not Gordon. My friend Phil Rawlins, who introduced us, told me what a terrific guy he is but that he gets asked to do things like this all the time, so expect him to be wary at first.

"Crikey, Mike," I said to myself, "you'd better be good; this is Gordon Banks, the greatest goalkeeper in history, the only British Keeper ever to lift the World Cup. This man has done what Peter Schmeichel, Petr Cech, Edwin van der Saar and Jens Lehmann between them have never done.

This man made the greatest save of all time, from Pelé himself. You'd better be good Mike. Don't let this bloke down." We agreed to do the full interview the following day.

Have you ever been excited and terrified at the same time? Perhaps that is what it feels like to walk out to play in a World Cup Final? *'I never thought about stuff like that when I was a kid. We had nothing, people had nothing at all – we just didn't have much, you know, and you had to look after yourself. We just kicked a ball for something to do and I now realise how much it helped me, especially playing on rough ground, where the ball was all over!'*

Was he a star goalkeeper at age seven, I wondered. *'Was I heck! Nobody wanted to go in goal, we took turns! I was a centre half. I only became a goalkeeper because we needed one rather than a centre half!'*

Does luck play a part? *'When I look back, luck or fate played a big part. I used to go watching (Sheffield) United or Wednesday and one day, when I was about sixteen, I missed the bus to the game, so went to the Rec instead to watch a game. A guy walked over who recognised me from school and told me I could play if I wanted as their keeper hadn't turned up, so I did – I went home to get some stuff but I didn't have any shorts, so I had to play in my trousers!'*

Gordon was an apprentice bricklayer at the time. *'I went for a trial with Rowmarch Welfare, who played in the Yorkshire League. In the two trial games I let in fifteen goals.'* **Oh dear, not the best start.**

'I was a bit disappointed **(a bit?)***, but it didn't bother me, I just thought I'd go back and play for the Millspaugh Steelworks team again. Next minute, Chesterfield came along for me and I thought, "this is a proper football club; they must think I'm alright."'*

They signed him as an Amateur and next minute he was playing for the Reserves at Old Trafford in front of 13,000 people. (Not in his trousers!) *'I was diving all over the place, it was like shooting practice for them! But I learned so much, even though I let a lot of goals in. I was teaching myself, there were no coaches for goalkeeping. I learned by playing and by watching the games at Sheffield, stood behind the goal, especially Bert Trautman, (the man who won an FA Cup Final with a broken neck!). We didn't have a training ground at Chesterfield, we just used to run around to keep fit.'*

The next step was being signed on as a full-time professional. Why did this make a difference? *'Because I could go back in the afternoon to the actual ground, and find somebody to bang balls at me, when* *everybody else had gone home. The Groundsman would only let me go in the corner, so I had no goals to work in! It was a bit difficult without goalposts.'*

It would be, wouldn't it! *'The year after, Leicester City came and signed me; they were in what we now call the Premier League. I couldn't believe it. I was twenty and getting paid a little bit more than I was when I was digging ditches. Yet, when I worked out all the hours I had spent, even in the dark, throwing a ball against a wall and catching it, outside in the light of the Co-op window, day after day, weeks on end, months at a time, year in, year out, no wonder I could do it! I could really see that ball.*

I used to copy the keepers I was watching too; Bert Trautman, for instance, was the first man ever to throw a ball out wide, so when I got in the team, I did it. I just watched and copied what I saw.'

When did the dream come alive then? *'When I played in the League Cup Final and the England Under-23 Team in the same season. I was doing a lot more training then at Leicester, because they did have a training ground and more players to wallop balls at me.'*

I asked him how he coped with mistakes or loss of form, not that the greatest of all time made mistakes. *'Oh I did, I made plenty, let loads of bad goals in, don't you worry. At one time, I even forgot how to take goal kicks, just kept duffing them! One of the Chesterfield Directors said something years before that really helped me, he said, "Look, if you make a mistake, the Golden Rule is, forget it, just put it out of your mind, because there's going to be another header or another shot coming in and if you're thinking about that last mistake, you'll make another one so just push it out of your mind." '*

Did Gordon see players suffer from nerves? *'Two of the lads at Stoke City used to throw up every week! There were players Alf (Ramsey) would pick for England who were playing brilliantly in the League but the England thing was just too big for them, the stage must have been too big. There was one lad from West Brom who came training with England and could do anything with a ball. He played once and I can't even remember his name!'*

What about Gordon though? *'Everybody has nerves! It must be the same if you're on a stage or whatever. But when that whistle went, I was fine. I think I was always a calm person, Alf liked that about me. I used to say to myself, "what is the point in getting anxious? Relax!" I used to go about things as if it was just a normal training session; that was my way.'*

I asked Gordon how much of his personal and team achievement was down to mental strength as opposed to being technically better than the opposition? His answer? *'All of it.'*

Wow! All of it? If Gordon Banks says it was 'all of it', then it was 'all of it'. *'Well, as your manager improves your team, you start to get a sense that you're a decent team, and that you can give people a game, whoever they are; your confidence builds, you know it, you feel it.*

You're going to play against special players in whatever game or sport, in my case it was the Brazilians; they were very special but I never let that intimidate me. When you get the feeling inside you, the confidence, you go for it. I always had my best games in front of the biggest crowds, places like Anfield, where their fans are behind you, shouting at you, and calling you all sorts. I would say to myself "I'll show you. You're not going to score past me." That used to fire me up even when they were winning everything, I wouldn't let them beat me.

The World Cup team had that confidence but remember, we were playing all over the world and winning games for quite a while. Each person was confident and Alf played a huge part in that. For instance, if two lads came from the same club and wanted to share a room together, there was no way; Alf would split them up, so you got to know people, know their lives and families, you'd sit and talk. It gave us this lovely feeling about each other; we went out to play for each other on the pitch.'

This all sounds quite a lot like the England Rugby team, before their World Cup in 2003, as it turns out.

Does Gordon have a final message for us? *'Never, ever give in when things go wrong. Remember, I am the lad who let in fifteen goals at his trial! Don't give in, keep trying. When I coached the Youth Team, I told the lads I was releasing them to go away and prove me wrong. I was making a decision but they were all good players, I could only pick one, so go and prove me wrong. Don't give in just because of what I say.'*

Gordon Banks, a man who is the greatest ever at what he did, has coached us today. What a gift; what a blessing; what, Gordon Banks or his wisdom? Both. He says *'I've been really lucky. Sport has been great to me.'*

Coach Says

1. Never give in; never let anyone be the final judge on you.
2. Practise, practise, practise.
3. Push mistakes out of your mind; another test is on its way.

You Say: write here your new decisions about how you will be more determined to win.

1. ....
....
2. ....
....
3. ....
....

You could try taking a leaf out of Gordon's book and don't give up.

When something goes wrong or goes against you, or when you make a mistake, how does it make you feel? Let me give you a few examples:

You miss an important putt at golf by no more than an inch or two.
You score a great goal and then are ruled offside.
You knock the high jump bar off with your heel.
You make a poor start to a race and end up losing.

Circle some of these feelings:

Angry   Frustrated   Disappointed   Upset
    Fed Up   Mad   Embarrassed   Intolerant
Dejected   Sad   Moody   Scared

Now, remember: Life is ten percent Fact and ninety percent Attitude. So the missed putt, the ref's decision, the heel or losing the race is only ten percent of the problem here – they are just 'facts' aren't they? Not everyone feels like you feel when those things happen to them and that is because **things mean different things to different people**.

Now here is the point: If the fact itself is only ten percent of the problem, the other ninety percent is Attitude – your Attitude. And how we get to feeling a certain way about a disappointment is by using what we call 'The Snap In' – we snap into feeling negative about something.

How do we do that? Simple, we use a 'catchphrase' and you will recognise that you actually have lots of them – negative ones!

Using negative catchphrases to 'snap in' results in us feeling negative. Obvious, eh?

So, what are your negative 'snap in' phrases? Here are some common ones I hear a lot!

'Oh no!' 'You must be kidding!' 'Why me!'
'For, God's sake!' 'What!!' 'Arghhhh!'
'I don't believe it!' 'No way!' 'What's the point!'

Now add your own, and no rude words!

....
....
....
....

You might recognise those – listen to people around you, and how they respond when something bad happens – it's funny to watch, unless it happens to you! It isn't very impressive though, seeing people lose their cool. Tennis player John McEnroe is probably the most famous and he recalls in his autobiography *Serious*, that he wishes he could have controlled himself better – he should have read this. He says that, with more control, he would have won many more championships than he did, and he did really well anyway!

The point is, you just don't need to feel like this, ever; it hurts your performance, you can't concentrate and you feel bad for days. Champions bounce back much more quickly, in fact, in seconds – just watch Tiger Woods next time he misses a putt.

Now, when you do have a problem, here are the feelings you need to have that will get you out of trouble, and back on track:

Inspired Determined Confident Focused

Creative Energised Patient Calm

Unbeatable Resilient Proud Excited

These feelings create the right response in us, almost instantly! So, how do we get there when something bad has happened? We use '**The Snap Out**'.

Here is what I hear people say to themselves when they realise how stupid and childish they are being just because something went wrong, and they want to 'Snap Out' of it:

'Come on, sort yourself out!'

'Oh, get a life!'

'Pull yourself together!'

'Move on; it's gone; it's over; forget it'

'Chill out!'

'Grow up!'

What are the 'Snap Out' phrases that you use?

....

....

....

....

....

....

Now, all I want you to do is recognise when you have used a 'Snap In' and replace it with a 'Snap Out' as quickly as you can; in fact, as soon as you realise what you have done.

How hard can this be?

I cannot tell you how many bookings it has saved us in Premier League football matches, how many penalties at Rugby League, how many shots in Golf and how many bad balls in Cricket, simply by getting players to learn to 'Snap Out' of bad moods more quickly than they used to!

Time yourself; be prepared to be amazed at the difference you can make to your performance and be ready to be praised for becoming a better leader and member of your team.

See if you can be like Master Yoda and never use negative 'Snap In' comments to yourself at all!

'Leads to the Dark Side; kill you it will,' he said to Luke!

Just to reinforce how important Attitude is, just read what South African cricketing legend Eric Simons has to say about it.

'I often wondered during my career as a professional cricketer why some cricketers made it at the level of first-class cricket and why some simply could not make the grade. The one thing that I knew to be true without any shadow of a doubt was the fact that it was not based on talent. I looked at the cricketers around me in the Western Province team and

even South African team and, while each one deserved to be there, we were not the most talented cricketers playing the game. I do not think I truly found the answer while I was playing and, even as I ended my playing career, the question remained largely unanswered. It was only when I started coaching and every member of the team became my responsibility, and when I started to really study and understand them, did I begin to realise what made the difference.

The first thing I learned was that one had to define what it meant to be successful. I realised there were cricketers I had played with and coached that, even though they may have played for their country, had never truly been successful. With the ability and talent they possessed they should have reached greatness but a flaw in their make-up meant that they were satisfied long before they had reached their potential. Then there were others who, by comparison, had limited ability and achieved far beyond their potential.

Duncan Fletcher, my coach while I was playing for Western Province, when asked whether a cricketer would make it at the highest level, would always reply that he could not tell by simply watching him play. He had to meet the person and understand his character. He said that you can put a limit on a cricketer with talent but you can never put a limit on a cricketer with guts.

In that answer lay the simple truth – sport is far more a test of character than it is a test of technique. When you walk out to bat in a Test Match in the final innings chasing 250 and your team is 90 for 5, when you need to sink a three-foot putt on the final green of a major championship to win the title, or if you need to take the catch to win the match that secures the club championship for your local club, what is going to be tested is your character and ability to deal with the pressure.

It is mental strength that determines your attitude.

There are five characteristics I have seen separate the good from the great.

1. The first is that they have a clear and definite stated goal for achievement.
2. They are extremely passionate in the pursuit of this goal.
3. Tough times and difficulties along the way are seen as opportunities and not threats.
4. When they mess up, they seek the solution internally – they do not play 'the blame game'.

"It is mental strength that determines your attitude."
Eric Simons - South African cricketing legend.

5. They keep their faith in themselves and their ability to overcome and succeed.

Unfortunately I learned how important these characteristics are relatively late in my career and, if I had it all over again, I would spend a lot more time building and developing them in myself so that they became far more a part of my DNA – part of the very fibre of the person I needed to be because, through them, true greatness is achieved.

You will notice that talent is not mentioned on the list. I have seen far more sportsmen succeed in spite of their lack of talent than I have seen sportsmen succeed because of their abundant talent.

When we were fielding and the chance of a catch came our way, we had a philosophy that you must make every effort to take the catch rather than pull out at the last minute through a fear of failure. It is probably one of the main reasons many talented sportsmen and women do not give themselves a real crack at the chance of glory – they fear failure. But the truth is that real failure is never having tried in the first place.

Do you know why Jonty Rhodes, South Africa's greatest ever fielder, took so many breathtaking diving catches? It is because when the chance came, he dived!

Life will only give you so many chances to do something breathtaking. In that moment when you need to make a decision, you either take the chance and dive or turn and fetch the ball from the boundary like most people do, and you will never know if you could have caught it.

Don't dive for someone else, don't do it for the glory, don't even do it because you can; do it because think you can't, do it because you owe it to yourself to push to a place you did not believe you could go.

Don't ever let your self-esteem be dependent on whether you succeed or fail, rather build it on your ability to face the challenge with a glint in the eye of someone that knows that real achievement lies not in conquering the mountain but in the way you approach the mountain.

How can it ever really be a challenge if you know you can achieve it – how can you be brave if you aren't scared?

The answer is clear. Success or failure will not be dependent on your ability to deal with the problem, it will depend on your attitude towards the problem.

Do it now!!'

Well there you have it from the top! Go for it.

Chapter Four

The Why Words

When things go against us in life, when we make mistakes, when people let us down or when we are just having a run of bad luck, it is SO easy to make things worse by having a real go at ourselves. I call this wrong use of 'The Why Words'.

Think about all the times you've had a situation when you've been your own worst enemy and used 'The Why Words' the wrong way. Look at these examples.

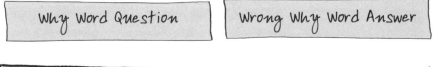

Why Word Question	Wrong Why Word Answer

Golf
You choose a six iron and then hit a bad shot

'Why did I do that?'	*Because you're an idiot'*
'Why can't I hit that six iron?'	*'Because you don't like it'*
'Why didn't I hit a seven iron?'	*'Because you always make the wrong choice!'*
'Why do I always mess things up?'	*'Because you just do!'*

Football
You have a great chance to score but take an extra touch and get tackled

'Why did I let that happen?'	*'Because you always take too long!'*
'Why didn't I just shoot?'	*'Because your touch is off'*
'Why can't I score those!'	*'Because you think too much!'*

> **Tennis**
> **You run to the net to volley the ball and put it into the net**
>
> 'Why now?'
>
> 'Why didn't I just hit it?
>
> 'Why wasn't it on my good side?'
>
> *'Because you can't do it when it counts!'*
>
> *'Because you're not confident on the shot and you know it!'*
>
> *'Because the opponent has sussed you out!'*

Now if you look at those ten comments we have made to ourselves, they are all negative, creating negative images, making us feel worse than we do already and sapping our confidence; every single one of them!

Just listen to us feeling all sorry for ourselves, getting really down on ourselves, and giving ourselves no chance whatsoever to get back in control.

Write a couple of examples of your own:

> ....
>
> ....
>
> ....
>
> ....
>
> ....
>
> ....

This is not acceptable and not a sign of mental strength; this is 'The Why Words' habit of a Loser!

The Winner develops a completely different Why Word habit. It is all based around positive reinforcement. Let me show you using the same examples.

| Why Word Question | Right Why Word Answer |

Golf
You choose a six iron and then hit a bad shot

'Why am I here?'

'Because I deserve to be and because I can really play this game!'

'Why did I play such a lousy shot?'

'Because I am learning, and that shot taught me something!'

'Why didn't I hit a seven iron?'

'Because nobody's perfect. Next time I will make a better decision because my decisions are good and getting better all the time!'

Tennis
You run to the net to volley the ball and put it into the net

'Why am I here?'

'Because I deserve to be and because I can really play this game!'

'Why didn't I just hit it?'

'I have to pull my socks up, hit the next one and, if I'm not comfortable, practise it for next time!'

We have to learn to stop using The Why Words wrongly, start to use them positively and make sure we have a lot of positive statements about ourselves ready to use when bad things happen.

Now, come on, turn your negative examples around.

```
.................................................................................................
.................................................................................................
.................................................................................................
.................................................................................................
.................................................................................................
.................................................................................................
```

In the heat of battle, the competition, at some point, will force you to take The Why Word Challenge.

You had better be ready.

Wrong use of The Why Words makes us give ourselves the wrong answers and that leads to tension, anger, fear, and even worse performance.

> *'When the training hurts and I'm feeling tired, I simply focus on why I'm doing it and think of the Olympics'*
> Reiss Beckford
> *British Gymnast, Gold Medallist, UK School Games 2005*
> *(BBC Sport, 27 January 2007)*

Good use of The Why Words leads to good answers, creating focus, belief and energy, and that leads to immediate improvement.

> *'Come on Young Jedi – Control!'*

A person who definitely has that control is Beth Tweddle. I just can't imagine her or her coach Amanda Kirby, ever using the wrong Why Words.

Beth was twenty-one when she became Britain's first ever World Gymnastics Champion, winning the Asymmetric Bars title in October 2006. She won the World Cup in the same discipline in Brazil in December 2006 and was third in the BBC Sports Personality of the Year.

"You meet ambitious people, don't you, but not Beth-ambitious."
-Amanda Kirby.
"Injuries are the worst... Once I had a cast on one foot, so I just put a weight on my other foot to even it up and got on the bars!!" - Beth Tweddle.

Her Coach, Amanda Kirby, was named Female Coach of the Year at the 2006 Coaching Awards and also won a prestigious Mussabini Medal (if you watch *Chariots of Fire* you will find out about Sam Mussabini).

The pair of them make a dynamic, ambitious, fun-loving, energetic, charismatic team, and they have, literally, conquered the world; but how?

Imagine you are going to meet a gymnast who just happens to be a double World Champion. You are going to her training headquarters where you are also going to meet a World Silver medallist and a British Junior Champion. Now, what do you think you will find in terms of the venue and the support team?

If you were in an Eastern European country or perhaps the United States, you could expect to find fantastic gleaming facilities and an array of coaches including nutritionists, physiotherapists, choreographers, fitness specialists, technical advisors and sports scientists, all lined up waiting to serve you. But no, this is Great Britain, where even World Champions have to 'make do'.

Here, in Toxteth, the training headquarters is hidden away, not for any reasons of secrecy but because the training headquarters is simply a public gym. As for the array of specialist coaches? Well, Beth Tweddle, Great Britain's first World Champion gymnast, does indeed have them, all of them, they are just all crammed into the one body which belongs to Amanda Kirby, her coach. Quite a trick that. You won't meet many people with the talent and drive to perform six or seven key roles so well they can coach a World Champion. "... and parent, and mentor, and teacher, and big sister ..." adds Amanda. Sorry, ten or eleven roles.

I spent a couple of mornings in this oasis, drinking in the professionalism, the dedication to excellence and the relentless pursuit of perfect performance. I came out of that gym ready to take on the world myself. It's a warm, safe, welcoming place.

The centre of the gymnastics universe is not in Moscow or Manhattan; it is in the city with two cathedrals, two Liver Birds, two football clubs and that was home to the world's biggest band of all time. It is very close to the centre, where litter, buses and people jostle for position and where scaffolding and road works tell you that something big must be happening; Liverpool is Capital of Culture 2008, and it's getting its make-up on.

'I've been teaching here for eleven years now,' says Amanda, the ultimate multi-tasker, 'and you don't meet many Beth Tweddle's in that time.'

I want to know why? What's so special about her? Is she just one of those rare natural talents that come along every so often?

'Well, you meet ambitious people, don't you, but not Beth-ambitious.' **(Wow, a new word for our dictionaries!)** *'It wasn't talent, and certainly not her physical stature that stood out when I met her,' Amanda explains, 'there was just something in her eyes, you can see it, and then there was the way she handled herself in her first competitions. Even recently on the BBC Sports Personality of the Year, she performed part of her World Cup routine, and it was the toughest test she has faced. She was as nervous as anything, but you couldn't tell and she did brilliantly; that's Beth. When she is competing, I watch the other gymnasts and when Beth finishes, they all just shake their heads and I know they are thinking "how does she do it?" She is amazing.'*

'Make sure they see you'

In the 1998 World Cup Final, the host nation, France, played the favourites Brazil in Paris. In the tunnel, as the teams waited to walk out, the French Captain, Didier Deschamps, turned to defender Marcel Desailly, one of the stars of the team. Deschamps who played in midfield for Juventus, had won every trophy in the game and was labelled an unspectacular but vital player.

'Marcel,' he said, 'the world is watching you.'

'I know Didier,' replied Desailly.

'Make sure they see you,' demanded Deschamps, quietly.

Deschamps was making sure that Desailly knew that this was his moment to shine, to step up, to stand up and be counted.

Beth loves the sport, Amanda explains. 'A break kills her! Over Christmas, she was texting me, asking me what time we were starting back in the New Year! I sent her a text back that told her to go to a party or something! That is just how she is. I have constantly to hold her back, constantly. She works six days a week, sometimes seven hours a day, and she just loves it. She's spoiled me really and made me realise that I only want to work with people who have that fire inside them. Years ago, you could get by on your talent *but now the routines are so physically demanding that you have to put the work in, so kids who will do the work can learn the routines. I'll take that desire over talent every time.'*

That's a pretty clear message.

'It's infectious too. Ash, the girl who has just come in, has had a tough eighteen months with injuries, but she took part in the British Championships and came third, after eighteen months off. When you come to this club now, excellence just seems to be expected. Even though we never demand it or talk about it, it just happens now.'

Success is in the air here and plastered all over the walls too. "I am always asking them to visualise success," says Amanda, "and I'm not sure that other coaches do, but when they're just chilling out, I'll say, 'Right, come on, we're in the British Championships, you know the venue, can you see it? Can you smell it? How do you feel?' I never did that when I was competing, so I like pushing them to do things I never did that I know will make a difference for them. They do it too. Then I'll ask them how it was and say "Was there a big cheer when you landed? What was the judge wearing?" They look at me and know they must do better next time. Eventually it just becomes second nature.'

> **The brain does not know the difference between a real and imagined experience.**

Does it work? *'One girl, a few years ago had a back injury for four weeks and all she could do was conditioning work, nothing on her technique, so we just did loads and loads of visualising and she came second in the British Championships. The next day in training she was a bag of shite but on that day, everything she visualised came off!'*

I am getting a real glimpse into Amanda's psyche here. She is talking to me but watching each move every girl makes and acknowledging them so they know, and she is doing it every single time any girl does something. I remember how good that felt, when my Coach watched just me and praised me in front of my mates. I asked her who she admires.

'Fergie; Sir Alex Ferguson. He has been so successful for so long, he is just awesome. I could learn from him. I would love to meet him, watch him work, ask him a few things.'

I point out that Fergie would not make any list of 'all time great players' and neither would Mourinho, Wenger or Benitez, so she may well be onto something. *'I bet he loves coaching as much as I do. With me it's unfinished business. I was never that good as a gymnast myself so I love using all the experience from whatever I got wrong to help others get it right. In 2002, our new Technical Director told me he thought our kids could do more so, thanks to him, I pushed them a lot harder and they responded.*

Fergie gets his people to give their best, no matter what the game. I think we do that too. We just go out to do our best, no matter what the competition, so our goals are process goals, not Championship ones. We put one hundred percent into everything here, training, club events, you name it, one hundred percent. Nobody gets away with anything.'

That's interesting as I have just watched Beth train hard for three hours and half of that time was upside down (her not me)! Beth comes over and Amanda leaves us to video a British Junior Champion on the Asymmetric Bars. Amanda has seen one foot half an inch out of line and she can't bear it. I turn around a minute later and she is showing Jenny the video she has recorded and am astonished to find them both looking at the screen on Amanda's phone. No expense spared in British Gymnastics, but they just get on with it, no moaning here.

Here is what Beth had to say. She's full on, bright, alert and sharp. *'Ever since I was young, Amanda has only ever asked me to go into a competition and produce my best performance. She never puts pressure on me by asking me to win, just to give my best performance. If that means I win a medal, I win a medal; but it does mean that I can always be happy with what I have done if I know I gave the best performance I was capable of.'*

Is that typical of her approach to goal setting? *'For us, baby goals work best. I look to the next competition, decide I want a perfect routine, then work on that for the next few months and think about nothing else.'*

So how does she cope with bad days? *'Injuries are the worst. I was a hyperactive kid,' she says, 'and so I loved bouncing around in here. I loved swimming too and I still love coming here so, even when I am injured I come in and do whatever I can. Once I had a cast on one foot, so I just put a weight on my other foot to even it up and got on the bars!'*

So, here is the big question, what makes a World Champion? *'A lot of determination. You can't let injuries or setbacks make you quit. Af-*

ter my injury at the Commonwealth Games in 2006, I was ready to pack it all in but the next morning I was fine. I will never give up something knowing I could do better. Sometimes you get bored with the training but then you look around and realise you are still winning, and still getting that buzz from competing. Then you're fine.'

Will she go on as long as the buzz is there? *'Definitely.'*

Is there an Olympic Gold and another World Championship in her destiny?

Check out Beth's website **www.bethtweddle.com**, and right at the bottom on her own diary page, it says

'Remember all you little or older ones out there, anything is possible.'

And what of Amanda, will she carry on coaching? *'I will be here as long as I still have The Eye.'*

I wouldn't bet against a few more highs for these superstars.

Coach Says

1. Give one hundred percent every single day, as if it was your last.
2. Visualise perfect performance.
3. Don't just be ambitious;
   be **Beth-ambitious!**

You Say:

1. ....

....

2. ....

....

3. ....

....

Look back one last time at what Reiss Beckford said he focuses on when he needs some inspiration. Just make sure that you can do the same. Find your own words of inspiration. I have and I use them many times, every single day. When you don't think you can take another step, your 'Why Words' will convince you that you can.

Chapter Five

The Reminder

Let's accept that we can all have a bad minute, a bad hour, a bad game, even a bad day, because we are, after all, only human.

> ***'You lost today kid but it doesn't mean you have to like it'***
>
> Indiana Jones and the Last Crusade

Fine, bounce back! But what happens if the bad run goes on too long? What if it goes on so long that you feel like it will never end and that you just can't go on? What if it all seems too much and you feel like giving up?

Let me tell you a little story here about a distance runner who ran really good times until the very last lap when he would lose the lead and easily lose the race. His coach asked him why this happened. "It's the bell Coach," the boy answered. "When I hear that bell and think there is still one more lap to go, I realise how much it hurts and it just saps my strength."

"Okay," said the coach, "next time you hear that bell, I just want you to stop running and sit down on the side of the track until the race is over."

"I can't do that!" replied the boy.

"Why not? If you're hurting, just stop."

"But what about my parents who pay for me to come here and give up so much so that I can run? What about my younger brothers who look up to me? What about all my friends who think I can win Gold at the Olympics? I would be letting them all down."

"Next time the bell rings, why don't you think about them," said the coach.

The coach was teaching the boy to use 'The Reminder'. What is it? Why does it work?

The Reminder is there to jog your memory about just exactly why you started down the path you have chosen. It allows you to think positively about all the talent you have, about all the sacrifices you have already made, about all the people who are behind you, helping you, about all the progress you have already made, and about all the great hopes and dreams you have for the future.

The Reminder *answers you* when you *ask yourself* 'What is the point of all this?' or 'Why am I bothering?' It is there to stop you feeling down.

The Reminder works because it releases all those great chemicals in the brain that make you feel better, energised, inspired, confident, determined, successful, unbeatable, focused, resilient, brave, enthusiastic and optimistic again.

Do you have a positive Reminder statement? If not, write one now.

Answer these questions:

My Reminder

Why am I doing this?

....
....
....
....

What are my goals?

....
....
....
....

They Did You Can

Who inspires me?

....

....

....

....

What would they say to me if they could see me right now?

....

....

....

....

Who is in my corner?

....

....

....

....

What do they think of me?

....

....

....

....

What makes me so good?

....

....

....

....

Why do I want to succeed?

....

....

....

....

What am I going to do when I achieve my really big goal?

....

....

....

....

How will I feel?

....

....

....

....

How will I celebrate?

....

....

....

....

Coach Says

1. Now, copy this out properly and keep it safely in the bag you use to carry your kit in.
2. Read it every time you are getting ready to go out and practise or compete.
3. Read it if you ever feel down. Keep it secret. Keep it safe.

A really good friend of mine is very good at keeping himself and those around him very firmly focused on what is important. When I first met him in 2003 he made a big impression on me and did an impression for me too.

You have never seen a Jack Nicholson impression until you have seen Gary Kirsten's Jack Nicholson impression. When did I see it? I saw it for the first time in July 2003 in the Visitors' Dressing Room at Lord's Cricket Ground in London. I was working with the South African Cricket Team during their five Test Matches against England. My job was to motivate the team and England were hot favourites to win. They didn't.

The match at Lord's was hailed as South Africa's greatest ever victory. Gary Kirsten played a huge part in it and then played a huge part in the party afterwards too! One of my most treasured possessions is a copy of the photograph which appeared on the front page of *The Times* newspaper, which is signed by the team and in which you can see one Englishman standing (me!) between all the South Africans celebrating on the famous balcony.

I am honoured to count Gary among my friends and my customers. His insights into how I helped him get to grips with the mental side of professional sport make for interesting reading.

Gary Kirsten retired as the leading run scorer in the entire history of South African Cricket. He is a fighter and a class act. *'I played sport every single day of my life from the age of four. That was how I grew up.'*

Sport was in his family and he told me that his older brother, Peter, was the talented one. *'I played any and every sport I could think of but cricket was the one I was best in the school at, so I suppose that was the one I thought I could be best at.'*

Did he think his talent would carry him through? *'No way! There was no way I thought I could go all the way just because of how good I was at school level. I was good at cricket at school but then I stagnated. I never became much better afterwards and I probably ended up not regarding myself as being that talented at all.'*

I asked him whether he thought he was good enough? *'At eighteen, nineteen, twenty, there were long periods of time when I thought "I'm going to have to go and do something else, I'm not going to be good enough to be able to make a living as a sportsman. I can't play this game." I was doing okay, but never thought I could really make it'.*

What changed? What happened to fight off this self doubt? *'Duncan Fletcher'.*

What? Our Duncan Fletcher, Regainer of The Ashes? *'Duncan became a big mentor to me. He instilled confidence in me.'*

What had happened was that, after a University game in which Gary played well, Duncan, the coach, was taking some of the team to the pub in his car. He held Gary back and asked him, "Do you think you can play at the next level?" Gary said that he didn't know. "Well, do you believe in yourself?' Gary's answer was that he wasn't sure and didn't know what he wanted to do with his life. "Well, you'd better get your act together, because I think that you can," said Fletcher.

'At that moment, I found somebody outside my family who really believed I could play. That one moment was huge. It gave me momentum. To have someone outside your circle say, "Look, I'm backing you," was huge for me.

Duncan and I have stayed in touch our whole lives but that was the one moment when he really kicked my arse into gear. It was a life-changing moment. I went to bed that night and remember asking myself, "What are you going to do about it?" I made a conscious decision to start taking my sport really seriously. I got fit and I practised, not twice a week but five times a week. Sure, there was sacrifice but I started acting like a professional and really putting in the hours.'

Within a year he was a professional.

I wondered what I had added to him when we met in the last two years of his career. *'Let's just say they were statistically the best two years of my entire career, by a long way!'*

He believes that people in professional sport look at the mental side and are scared to go there. *'I gained an understanding of my mental processes that I had never had before. It was a totally new level and you gave me tools to apply in the heat of battle at the very highest level, in the most pressurised situations.'*

> **Did it work? Well I reckon it did as Gary, as a batsman, averaged over 60 runs every time he went out to bat in those two years. There is only one man playing the game today who does that; Mike Hussey for Australia. Just one man; that's how special Mr Kirsten was.**

" You want the truth? You cant handle the truth ! "
His favourite Jack line.
'' Dont get mad, get even ! ' one of his own.

GARY KIRSTEN: 'The Saviour'. Scored 275 runs.
A South African record.

'In the past, when I was walking out in front of 40,000 people, where guys were waiting to throw missiles at me at one hundred miles an hour, I would fight my emotions. You taught me not to fight them, but instead to say, "Hey, so I'm nervous, so what? I can still perform!" And I did.'

Professional sport brings pressure if you want to do well, you won't escape that but it doesn't have to beat you. 'All the way through my career I lacked self belief to a large degree. I went through many periods when I thought I wasn't good enough even when I had played for my country seventy times! I was never touted as being "the next big thing", you know, I fought my way through the whole time.'

Gary believes that young people making their way in sport need to hear that their heroes went through the mill too, that they weren't perfect as that is how it may look to other people. 'Young people don't want to hear how great you were because they know that; nineteen year olds don't have a clue if you talk about your success because that is not where they are! They want to hear about how you struggled because that is exactly what they are going through. I love telling young people about when I felt like I was useless, about when I felt vulnerable, about when I felt like I wasn't good enough. I want to teach them to fight against all that; prove people wrong. I felt really vulnerable for most of my career but I learned how to fight, even though I felt like a dog!'

Young people will find it really difficult to open up to their vulnerability in the egotistical world of professional sport. He warns that you can't tell your coach as you won't play in the next game, so you hide it. You have to find people who can help you; so get good people around you, people who see your qualities, who will let you talk and listen to you, and help you focus on your positives. Your ability to understand yourself is everything, everything! You have to learn to master your fear.'

But is the fear in a tough sport only physical?

'Not at all. What I see a lot is not the fear of failure, because that never leaves you, but the fear of success. You have to have a passion for your sport. People will achieve success in whatever they have a passion for. You have to find something in this life that fires you, something that you want to eat, sleep and breathe. So many people go through life being happy with mediocrity. I never wanted to be mediocre; I wanted to be bloody good at whatever I chose to do. It's easy to go through life in sport and do okay financially and avoid the pressure, but if you want to be the best, win gold medals or championships or represent your country, you have to overcome fear of success. Lots of people are afraid of success because then *you are under the microscope, putting yourself under intense pressure. Some people just cannot cope with that, no matter how talented they are. It's about pride, Boy, pride in yourself and pride in your performance.'*

Gary spent his sporting life from the age of eleven being told he was only in teams because of his older brother, Peter. *'It made me want to prove them all wrong, right through my career and it served me well in 2000, when the press were on my case saying I was too old and no good any more so I just said to myself, "I'll show you, and when I go big, boy, I am going to go big and shove this right back down your throat."*

And what happened? He scored 275, a South African record, and was hailed as 'The Saviour'.

Who said, 'don't get mad, get even'?

'Life's great lessons come from situations that are tough,' says Gary, *'where people struggle, that's when you find out about yourself.'*

And what message would he pass on to future generations of sporting hopefuls? *'It's okay to be vulnerable; learn to understand yourself and the processes you go through when you are under pressure and learn how to deal with it. Pressure then becomes irrelevant, because it is just always there.'*

So just use your reminder to keep you on track about your success. Remember that one line that perhaps someone told you when you were losing heart, just like Gary did when his coach said he believed in him.

Coach Says

1. Wanna be a professional? Fine. Act like one – now.
2. Only do it if you're passionate about it – passion guarantees success.
3. Don't like criticism? Learn to thrive on it.

You Say:

1. ....
   ....
2. ....
   ....
3. ....
   ....

You don't have to be the best to get to where you want to go but you do have to be mentally strong and remind yourself why you have committed yourself to great goals and dreams. Courage will carry as far as you need to go.

'He imagined the feel of the tape at the winning line crossing his chest and breaking, a picture and a feeling he had been through many times in his mind.'
Linford Christie won Gold at the age of 32, in under 10 seconds. Magic!!

Chapter Six

Part One

The Moments of Magic

Linford Christie stood on the start line in the final of the 100 metres at the Olympic Games in 1992, closed his eyes and imagined the feel of the tape at the winning line crossing his chest and breaking, a picture and feeling he had been through many times in his mind. He won Gold. He was thirty-two. Before him, the oldest man to win had been twenty-eight. It was the only time in that whole year that Christie had run under ten seconds. Magic!

'The race does not always go, to the stronger or faster man,
For, sooner or later, the one who wins is the one who thinks they can'

Anon

What have been the very best moments of your entire life so far? Can you recall them? Can you remember how they made you feel and can you relive the experience? Are the pictures the pictures of what happened still in your mind? Can you still hear the sounds or sense the movements that were going on? How do you feel now that you have just been thinking about them?

They Did You Can

Come on, follow my example. Write some down now.

The Moment	What I can see
2000 Play Off Final, Bolton v Preston	Ball hits the net for 2-0 and I hug the nearest person

When I do this, I think of many things that get forgotten in the rush or when times are hard.

This is another list I want you to carry with you in your bag. If you ever feel low, I want you to read this. You will instantly feel better because you are remembering how great your life has been at times, how well you have done, how fortunate you are and how brilliant you are.

Remember, INTENSE thoughts, repeated often, create better patterns of behaviour and the better you feel, the better you'll be!

If you find this exercise difficult, it just means that you need to spend a little more time focusing on your successes and remembering the good

What I hear/feel	How I feel now
Cheers, relief, joy then it sinks in, 'we made it!'	Immensely proud, tall, strong, special
....	....
....	....
....	....
....	....
....	....
....	....
....	....
....	....
....	....
....	....

times. Set yourself a goal to have at least five great memories to look back on and even more if you can.

Our aim is to spend as much time as we possibly can feeling good and as little time as we possibly can feeling bad.

 **Come on, work at this, you're worth it!**

Part Two

The Power of GDB

Now look, I am about to explain to you, the greatest secret that was ever revealed to me:

It's about Goal, Desire and Belief.

When I learned to master the second part of what I call **'Moments of Magic'**, I finally started to achieve my true potential. I also learned how to develop that potential so that I could start dreaming of achieving things that, previously, I would have thought to be beyond me.

This mind stuff is simply awesome in what it will do for you, if only you will let it!

In Moments of Magic, Part One, you showed that you have developed the ability to recall powerfully the moments from your past when you achieved things you are proud of.

Now let's just remind ourselves here of a few of the vital pieces of information we have learned together.

1. The human brain finds it almost impossible and highly irrelevant to distinguish between something which is happening that is real and something we are only imagining. Remember that?

2. When the brain does this, it releases chemicals which, in turn, reinforce dendrites by travelling along them. Remember that?

3. Dendrite formation is driven by the application of two variables; intensity and frequency. Remember that, too?

Now think for a minute or two about a significant goal that you achieved. Write it down; in fact write down the stories of three goals you

What did you do that someone else could follow to achieve their own goal? Let's see.

1. Goal

You knew exactly what you wanted and could explain it to yourself clearly in lots of different ways. You could see yourself doing it.

2. Desire

You really wanted to do this so badly it hurt! You thought about it all the time, you obsessed about it, you dreamed about it. You were thinking about it even when other people thought you were just watching television. You could not get it out of your mind.

3. Belief

You actually even believed you could really do it; in fact, you never doubt-ed it and this meant that, when you made mistakes or hit some kind of brick wall, you just kept on going. You were relentless. You didn't care how hard it was going to get as you were not prepared to give up on your dream and you were going to make it happen!

Am I right? You bet I am, Bucko! That formula is pure magic, my friend! That formula is possibly the most powerful piece of knowledge you will ever come across – ever!

This is the knowledge that, if you know what you want and are prepared to make the necessary sacrifice, you can have it. Possibly the greatest book I ever read contains this next quotation. The book is all about what has been known since ancient times as 'the law of attraction', which is exactly what we are learning about now.

> **'It is your rightful heritage, your birthright, to have anything that you desire, without limit'**
>
> Message of a Master John McDonald, New World Library

Think back on those successes and answer these questions:

Did you always have the unswerving support of all those around you? NO!

Did people doubt you and write you off? YES!

Did you care what they thought? NO!

Did you have all the resources you needed at your fingertips? NO!

Did you let that put you off at all? NO!

Did you let anything derail you or deny you? NO!

Did you make excuses for yourself? NO!

Did you miss practice or lose focus or intensity or hope? NO!

Were you highly skilled in all aspects of what you were attempting? NO!

Were others around you more skilled? YES!

Did that bother you, intimidate you or stop you?	NO!
Had you ever achieved this thing before?	NO!
Did that stop you?	NO!

Why?

Because you had the Goal, the Desire and the Belief and that made you unstoppable, unbeatable, invincible. You made yourself into a machine. You could not be denied.

That formula is powerful enough to enable you to make any dream that you have come true. Why?

You didn't know it then but what you were really doing that enabled you to be successful was building dendrites, even though you had never actually done these things before! Once you have built that dendrite, you are on your way and the world had better watch out. No matter what it tries to put in your way, you are like The Fantastic Four and the X Men all rolled into one!

And guess what? If you can do this for one thing, you can do it for another, and another and another!

And remember it works for you as an individual OR as a member of a team.

I asked Martin Johnson for his thoughts on this, and just look what he said, the great leader who became the first man in history to lead a team from Great Britain and win the Rugby World Cup in 2003 with Sir Clive Woodward.

'Mike, people do often ask me what sort of Churchillian speech I delivered at the end of full-time and prior to going out for extra time at the Rugby World Cup final back in 2003. They ask me how was I able to motivate a team of guys who had just had the trophy cruelly snatched away from them with just a few seconds to go of normal time.

Whilst I would love to go into great detail about how I rallied the guys and picked them up off the floor, to do so would be plain wrong. There were no big speeches, no brow beating and no rallying of the troops. And I guess this in a nutshell is one of the reasons why I agreed to be in your book.

Mike, you repeatedly talk about the importance of belief and focus and I think these are the words that would encapsulate that five-minute talk before starting extra time.

Just looking around the circle and into the eyes of the guys, I instinctively knew at that point, we were going to win. They were a superb group of individuals, who had built up a huge sense of belief over the years through trust and confidence in each other. This sense of belief ensured we would be focused on what was needed to make sure the game was won.

Mike, you also say that talent alone is not enough and you are absolutely right. What that squad of guys had was a huge amount of talent coupled with a fierce belief and an unwavering commitment to focus on the job in hand.

And that is why on that incredible night we were crowned World Champions!

Did Martin and his Rubgy Team have a 'Goal' do you think? Did they have the 'Desire' to make that Dream come true? Did they have the 'Belief' that completes our magic formula? No doubt whatsoever. Thanks Martin.

You have no limits on what you can achieve. What the heck are you waiting for?

But wait a second here, I almost forgot. I have told you what to do (use the power of Goal, Desire and Belief in your life for anything you want to achieve in the future) but I have not told you how to do it. Let's put that right, now.

Okay, ready?

1. Get hold of some small cards, small enough to fit into a pocket, a wallet or a purse, maybe the size of a credit card or better still the size of a playing card. You are going to use both sides of the card and you are going to need one card for each goal you are going to set yourself. If you can't find any to buy, then make some.

2. Take one side of the card and write in the top corner the word 'GOAL' in big letters. On this side of the card you are going to write down exactly what the goal is that you want to achieve. Spell it out in clear, simple, specific terms. Write a date on the card when you want to have done this by.

3. Turn the card over. Now write on the top corner of this side 'INSPIRATIONAL DREAM'. This is the magic within the magic, the part that people really do not understand correctly at all. What you are now going to do is describe a 'Moment of Magic' but it will be one that has not yet happened. It will be the one that converts the goal on the other side of the card into your Inspirational Dream.

4. You are now going to create a picture in your mind, complete with sound, colour and feeling, that describes the 'Moment of Magic', the minute when the goal you have written down has come true, just as if it has happened. You are going to describe your picture using words on the card that come into your mind following a few simple rules.

    a. You are going to write them down as if the Moment is happening now or has just happened.

    b. You are going to use words that make the hairs on the back of your neck stand up or give you goose bumps, or make you clench your fist, or make you smile, or maybe all of these!

    c. You are going to make sure that the picture you describe matches exactly the goal written down on the other side of your card.

5. Secretly, you are going to keep this card close by you at all times. You are going to carry it in a pocket, purse, wallet, file or whatever.

6. You are going to read both sides of this card every day at least three times.

7. Each time, you are going to:

    a. **Read the Words, then**

    b. **See the Picture, then**

    c. **Feel the Emotions**

When you do this, the 'Emotions' you 'Feel' are a result of the brain releasing chemicals which are the proof that you have just built the dendrite which will enable you to achieve your goal.

Now remember, this is Miracle Grow and the formula to remember is **'Intensity x Frequency'** so, although you feel great, the performance might take a little longer to improve. That is normal. When the dendrite you have been building is finally fully constructed, the performance you were dreaming of will be yours. Remember, this is exactly how you learned to walk, to ride a bike, to swim and even to repeat your times tables. Remember,

'Repetition is the mother of skill'

For each goal you set for yourself you must have a card. Let's have a look at some examples showing how you might write down a 'Goal', and then turn it into an 'Inspirational Dream'.

Goal	Dream
Run a marathon in 3 hours 50 minutes 1st March 2009	I have just crossed the line at the London Marathon. The clock showed 3.49.56 and I feel fantastic!

Goal	Dream
Win a Gold Medal in the 2012 Olympics	I am standing on the top step of the podium. My medal is round my neck, the national anthem is playing. My family is waving at me, some of them so proud they are in tears.

Can you see how the 'Goal' describes your target very specifically and the 'Dream' brings it to life to bring you inspiration? Magic!

> **'Whatever you can dare or dream, begin it; boldness has mystery, magic and genius in it'**
>
> Goethe

Steve McManaman says that, as a child, he regularly used to pretend he was playing in the Champions League Final, scoring a goal and winning it with Real Madrid. He did it too, even though he was born and grew up on Merseyside! That was his 'Inspirational Dream'.

> **'It's the repetition of affirmations that leads to belief. And once that belief becomes a deep conviction, things begin to happen'**
>
> Muhammad Ali

Still, I think the best story of all in relation to the power of the Inspirational Dream belongs to Mary Peters.

When you meet champions, true champions, there is something about them that is different. With Mary Peters it is calmness, serenity, warmth; not always qualities we associated with Belfast back in the 1970s at the height of 'the Troubles' but then this lady is special.

Mary Peters won Gold in the Pentathlon at the 1972 Olympic Games in Munich, Great Britain's only Track and Field Gold of the entire Games. "It was my last chance at Gold," she explained. "I was thirty three and most people retired from my sport in their mid-twenties, and still do!"

Mary had already been to two Games, 1964 in Tokyo and 1968 in Mexico. *'I was fourth in Tokyo and ninth in Mexico but I kept going because I loved it.'*

From ninth to first is quite a leap, proving that dreams come true, but what changed? *'Understandably, looking at my results at the highest level, I never really thought I was all that good, but for that last year leading up to Munich, when I knew it would be my last chance, I really did decide that I just had to have Gold and that nothing else would do.'*

She picked a fine time to get ambitious! At thirty-three she was not ranked high enough to win any medal at all and she was going to the home country of the World Number One and red hot favourite, Heidi Rosendahl. The odds were well stacked against her. *'They were, but on the morning of the competition, I met Heidi's coach who was a really nice guy, and he said, "Mary, you are favourite; Number One," and by then, I knew he was right. If everything went right, there was nobody in Munich who was going to beat me. I had changed my attitude totally because I had had a long and varied career and I wanted to finish on a high.*

All the journalists were looking at me and thinking how confident I looked but they didn't believe I could do it.'

Still, everything didn't go right. *'First, my coach had back problems and I had to sort out his treatment. I had problems sleeping, I had problems with my shoes, I was drug tested on both days, I had had an Achilles injury, I had to go overdrawn at my bank to fund my training, I got confused on start times for events, you name it, but nothing was going to stop me. Even the running track where I trained was full of pot holes and, of course, in Northern Ireland it rains all the time when you're trying to* *train!'* **Mary was also working twelve-hour days at the time and training on top of that.**

She had to get away and went overdrawn at the bank to fund a six-week scholarship trip to California. It worked a treat. What happened when she came back reminded me of what Gordon Banks said about the England team in their build-up to 1966 and what Sir Clive Woodward reminds us happened with the Rugby Union team. She and they just got better and better and built real momentum as the championships approached. *'I competed in three events before Munich and every performance was better than before I had gone away. I really did go Munich very confident, though my coach and I pretty much kept it to ourselves.'*

Was it any wonder then that, in the five Pentathlon events, she produced three personal bests? *'Well, I got off to a great start, because the first event, the 100 Metres Hurdles, was one of my favourites; nobody really watches when you are doing the Shot Put but everyone loves a race, so the crowd was great and I ran my guts out! They wouldn't let me run in my new Puma shoes either but I had a pair of my old spikes in my bag, so I ran in those.*

I was on a high then but had to hang around in a warm-up circle for quite a while with all the other girls waiting for the Shot Put. I noticed that the three German girls weren't there, so I told my coach and he sorted that one out; they were in a private circle, just the three of them, whilst we were all in one big area together. They were brought back straight away. You see, psychologically, I was in that winning mindset, there was a real edge to me.'

No matter what the world threw at her, she was going to win that Gold. *'You're right, and that was so unusual for me because normally I am such a sensitive person but, for those two days, I was so intense. In the Shot Put, I recorded my best distance in competition ever, that's how focused I was and, remember, by then I was thirty-three!*

Then it was the High Jump. A year earlier I had changed my style and started to use the Fosbury Flop. That was a huge gamble at such a late stage in my career, especially as I was not a talented High Jumper. When the bar reached five feet six inches, I knocked it off. The second time I knocked it off again, so had only one attempt left and my coach was going crazy in the stands, telling me with hand signals to stay warmed up until my last attempt. Third time I got over, and from then, especially when Heidi

Mary Peters won Gold in the Pentathlon 1972 Olympic Games in Munich.
Finally she hung her medal on the wall of her hotel room, aged 33. She used a nail given to her in 1964 by Mary Rand and Ann Packer.

went out, I really kicked on. I ended up jumping six inches higher than I had ever jumped before! The Brits in the crowd went wild!'

Where did that performance come from? *'The desire to win'* said Mary, who had recorded the highest first day points total ever. I told her this: *'Oh, really, I never knew that. I just knew that I was well ahead of Heidi but that her strong events were still to come and that stopped me sleeping.'*

Heidi jumped out of her skin in the Long Jump, and her coach worked out that Mary would have to run faster than she had ever run in the final event, the 200 Metres, to win Gold. Not good. She had the whole day to wait. When she got back to her room, she just broke down crying. One of the girls asked what was wrong, and said, "What are you worried about, you're guaranteed a medal now!"

"I know," Mary answered her, *"but I don't want just any medal, I want the Gold."*

'Second place still has no appeal for me. I would argue that most champions have that mindset. In order to be truly successful in any endeavour, you have to adopt a no-fear attitude. Don't be afraid to go for it.'

Tiger Woods

In 1964 at the Tokyo Games, Mary had roomed with two other girls who arrived before her. When she got to the room, they were giggling and messing around. There was plaster on the floor from the wall. Mary wondered what on earth they were doing. "Sorry, we were just trying to knock these nails into the wall with this toffee hammer," they explained.

Can you work out what the nails were for? Mary asked them. Do you think they answered "to hang our medals on, of course"? Wrong.

"To hang our GOLD medals on," was the answer. "Oh, and here, we knew we were sharing with a third person, so we brought one for you too."

The girls then hurried out to their training session, leaving Mary alone in the room with her nail and the hammer. She never knocked the nail into the wall. She came fourth in her competition. She knew deep down that she wouldn't need any nail. The other two girls needed theirs though; they were Mary Rand (800 Metres) and Ann Packer (Long Jump).

They both won medals; GOLD medals; the first two Gold Medals ever won by British Women in Track and Field.

'I did keep my nail though,' said Mary. 'It went to Mexico with me but never got hammered in there either!' Oh dear. 'But when I got to Munich, as I unpacked my case, I took out my make-up bag and there inside was the nail and the hammer and into that wall it went. Maybe at thirty-three I wasn't the best athlete in my competition but I thought I was.'

> **'What lies before us and what lies behind us are tiny matters compared to what lies within us'**
>
> Ralph Waldo Emerson, American Author and Philosopher

Wow!

In that final race she produced her final personal best and won her Gold by just ten points with a total of 4801; a new world record.

> **'The winning margin may have been only 0.38 seconds, but in ten years' time, nobody's going to say, "Well, they only just won," What people will say until the day we die is, "They were Olympic champions"'**
>
> Sir Steve Redgrave

'It took an age to work out who had won as there were no computers in those days but I knew I had when Heidi walked over and shook my hand.'

> **'Champions aren't made in gyms. Champions are made from something they have deep inside them – a desire, a dream, a vision. They have to have last minute stamina, they have to be a little faster, they have to have the skill and the will. But the will must be stronger than the skill'**
>
> Muhammad Ali

Was it worth it? She didn't know that her Dad had come all the way from Australia to watch her and it was the first time he had ever watched her live. *'He was so proud, it was fantastic and life has been fantastic ever since.'*

What does this great lady think it takes to be a Champion? *'You have to want it badly, you have to be hungry.'*

Coach Says

1. Never think it is too late to improve.
2. Build your dream like Mary did, and make it non-negotiable.
3. Never make excuses, just make sure that setbacks make you more determined!

Can you write down three things that you've learned from this chapter?

You Say:

1. ....
....

2. ....
....

3. ....
....

I said at the beginning of this chapter that the power of **GDB** was the most influential thing I ever learned. I hope that this chapter has enabled you to learn it too so that you can reap the benefits and rewards that I have. If you, as Athlete, don't like what you've written, change it to something you feel will work for you. Keep working on it until you're happy with it.

Matthew Pinsent.
Four Olympic gold medals.
Enough said.

Chapter Seven

The Right Track

In 2005 I met Matthew Pinsent for the first time at Warwickshire County Cricket Club. We were both speaking, along with William Hague, the former Conservative party leader (who was hilarious by the way), at a conference for the Professional Cricketers' Association.

Matthew's speech was brilliant. It was all about working together as a team, about making sacrifices to achieve great things, respecting other people, setting goals and about trusting yourself and trusting each other.

He then did something really powerful. He took out a slim box, opened it and held it up to the audience of around 300 people. Inside were his four Olympic gold medals. They shone under the lights. The audience gasped. Then he did something amazing. He took them out of the box, walked down from the stage into the audience and handed out the four medals to four different people, none of whom he knew, and asked them to pass them along so that everyone could hold at least one.

He had just been talking about trust and, then and there, with probably his most prized possessions, he demonstrated it. He proved that he believed in trusting people. He made us all feel special. He got them all back too. Why wouldn't he? He was on 'The Right Track'.

Emile Zatopek was possibly the greatest distance runner of all time. In the 1952 Olympics, he won Gold in the 5,000 Metres, the 10,000 Metres and the Marathon, a feat which has not and will not be matched.

Years later, another great runner came along. He was an Australian called Ron Clarke. Clarke set eighteen world records but never won Olympic Gold. When Zatopek was an old man, Clarke went to visit him at his home in Czechoslovakia. When he left, Zatopek gave him a small package, a gift. "Promise me you will only open this when you are on the plane." When Clarke was on his plane home, he remembered the gift, took it from his pocket, and opened it. Inside was one of Zatopek's Olympic Gold Medals, with an inscription. "You were a great athlete and a great man.

Fate decided you would not win the Gold you deserved, so please, make an old man happy and accept one of mine."

Zatopek was not only a great athlete, he was a great human being. Zatopek was humble. He was on 'The Right Track' too.

He was quite the opposite of Canadian Ben Johnson who in 1988 won Gold in the 100 Metres but was stripped of his medal for taking drugs. He was definitely on 'The Wrong Track', especially as he could probably have won fairly and squarely without cheating.

So what about you? Are you on 'The Right Track'? Do you demonstrate by your actions that you are more than just a kid who likes sport? Is that all there is to you?

Early in my career, working with great sports people like Andrew Flintoff, Darren Clarke and even Jimmy White, I learned that, for them to win, they had to be right, on and off the field. I also learned that when they were not winning, often the cause was nothing to do with their sport.

When you work with elite athletes, you soon learn that they are pretty good at what they do and that most of the time you end up talking to them about things that are nothing to do with their sport but everything to do with their life.

I want you to think what you are like outside your sport. I want you to think about your life in five parts.

Fun: how much fun you have living your life

Friendships: how good your relationships are with family and friends

Future: how you are planning for success in the long term

Fitness: how well you are looking after yourself

Foundations: how well you would do in the Pinsent/Zatopek test. What are your morals?

Give yourself a score out of 10 against each. The question is 'How well am I doing right now in this area?' (1 would be a low score, 10 would be highest).

When you have five scores add them up. Now multiply the number by two. You now have a percentage score on how well you are developing as an all round person, not just a sports person.

Example:	
Fun:	5
Friendships:	7
Future:	6
Fitness:	4
Foundations:	4
Score:	26
x 2 = 52% on the PZ Scale	

So how do you improve? Take a look at this drawing.

Each area has three bubbles around it. In each bubble, write just one idea of a thing you could do to improve your score. These should be really simple things as shown in the example.

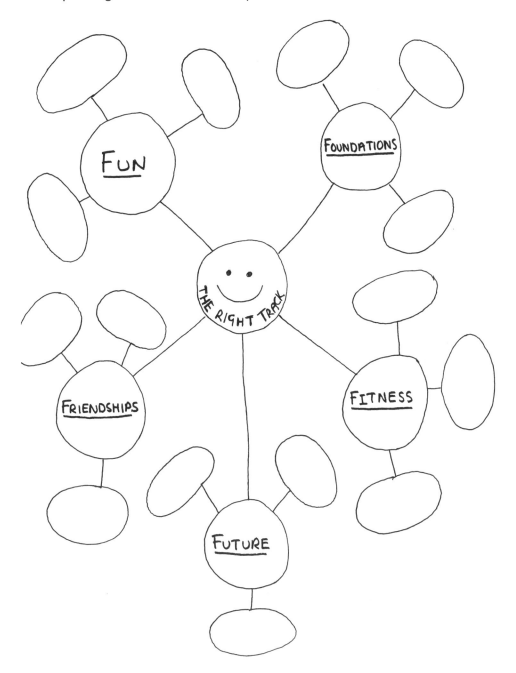

Each month I want you to look at your picture and see how many of them you have done during the month. Let's hope that, when you score yourself again after three months, you will have improved.

You want to reach the top in Sport? Good, then stay on 'The Right Track'!

I found a great example of this when I was talking to England International Cricketer and Leicestershire Captain, Jeremy Snape, who has won every major One Day Cricket Trophy including, uniquely, three in one season.

Jeremy Snape is a totally engaging character. When you first meet him, you can just tell that his handshake is going to demolish you but, at the same time, there is a sense of warmth to him that you just do not get from many people.

Jeremy is going to be a good guy, you think, but no pushover. *'Resilience, that's what sets apart the people I grew up with in cricket, who did or didn't make it.'*

You're not surprised by the answer; he looks resilient. He looks like a guy who believes in himself; who has had to fight for his success. I asked him what I should do if I interviewed a person for the book who proved to be 'perfect'. *'Just don't put him in. Everyone's human'.*

Easy to forget that, when you're there struggling to come to terms with your demons. Everyone really is human. *'I saw Gordon Banks speak at a dinner recently and he was asked what the feeling was when the whistle blew at the end of his World Cup Final. "Relief", he said. Even the great Gordon Banks felt the pressure to deliver.'* **Wise words indeed.**

It wasn't like that for Jeremy in his early years. His family was not a sporting one, the teams he played for were always underdogs, even when he was playing as a professional, and there were no expectations for him to fulfil. His Dad only took him to play cricket when he was eleven so that he could get on with the decorating.

Winning changed all that though. *'Early successes mean that people expect you to win then all you can think about is not losing, not making mistakes. Some players just couldn't handle the kind of pressure to make the step up whereas, before they were mentioned as England material, they were playing great.'*

Jeremy Snape: 'a good guy, but no pushover.'

Within four years of first playing cricket I captained the England Under-15s, to the huge surprise of my entire family. I was in the bottom three in terms of talent. Seventeen years later only I and one other guy made it, and the other guy was Ashley Giles, who at the time was an outstanding fast bowler. The guys with the most talent just couldn't handle the setbacks when things didn't work out their way. They wouldn't or couldn't reinvent themselves to cope with what was going on and they just kept on doing their thing because they thought that their thing was always going to be good enough.

The successful people kept adapting and were self aware. They knew their strengths and weaknesses, took on information and worked out what they were going to use.

Resilience is the key. You'll get injuries, you'll get performance setbacks, conflict with coaches, press and crowds creating pressure, and it's the guys who can't respond to that who fall by the wayside.'

> *'Only a man who knows what it is like to be defeated can reach down to the bottom of his soul and come up with the extra ounce of power it takes to win when the match is even'*
>
> Muhammad Ali

I wondered how Jeremy coped in those situations. *'I surrounded myself with people I respected and who had a balanced approach, and not from sport.'* **He would ask questions, listen to their perspective and be open with them about his fears.**

> *'The bad times. That's when you need a family'*
>
> Roy Keane
>
> (Sunday Times Magazine, September 2006)

He clearly remembers failing a school entrance exam he was expected to pass aged eleven and how he felt he had let down his family as they had all expected him to pass. *'I promised myself that I would work harder than anyone else was prepared to and would deal with* *things better than anyone else was prepared to, in order to put that right and to prove that I could be good at something.'*

Somebody just happened to put a cricket ball in his hand. With Muhammad Ali, it was the stealing of his bike that defined his life. The policeman he complained to told him he had better learn to fight if he was going to 'whup' those guilty of the crime and showed him into the local boxing gym. *'I sensed their disappointment and decided I was not going to have that again. That made me want to be as good as I can be in whatever I am doing.'*

He's still like that he says, and he is never totally satisfied with where he is. *'It's a journey. I mean, when do you really know that you've made it; is it as England Under-15s Captain, is it when you get a professional contract, is it when you make your debut for the first team, is it your first Man of the Match in a big game, is it your first England call up, is it when you get on the plane for an England Tour, is it when you first put the England shirt on? I never stopped at those because I always had aspirations to be better than I was at that minute. They were all just markers.'*

I pointed out that not all people see it that way. *'Well it depends where you set your sights. I just always keep thinking about getting better, looking forward, not back.'*

Did he just live for sport though? Was that crucial? *'The opposite; early in my life, my sporting CV was impressive but my life CV was not. I have always been happiest when my life is balanced with studies, friends, hobbies or business interests. It's all linked. The more I challenge myself the happier I am.'*

Would more support with the mental side of the game have helped him in his younger days? *'We coach too much technical skill and not enough about having the attitude to keep using your skills consistently. That is the reason people haven't made it; it's as simple as that. Michael Vaughan says cricket is ninety percent mental; Glenn McGrath said the same, so why don't we spend ninety percent of our time on that then? We keep going through the same technical things but then, under pressure, we have to learn to react to it.'*

How did Jeremy cope with his lowest moments? *'My biggest mistakes and setbacks have been my biggest learning experiences. Having Brett Lee break my thumb in Australia just before the World Cup was crushing; but then the next day I went for a run to keep up my fitness and tore my calf muscle. I was, literally, sitting in the gutter, feeling like a broken man, wondering where it had all gone wrong, but I just had this* *philosophical dawning that I had done all I could and could not have done anything differently. I got to that point fairly quickly thanks to the support I had around me.'*

Did he ever think he wasn't good enough? *'All through my career! It might have held me back but it gave me my work ethic. I've had it all and it makes you stronger. The high points make it worth it; Man of the Match on my international debut, the treble in one season, the friendships, the travelling, finding out about yourself on the journey, that's the best bit. I've been very lucky.'*

His final thought. *'If you really want to be better, then you have to get new information to make you better, so speak to people, don't be ashamed or afraid to ask people for help.'*

Coach Says

1. Never let setbacks put you off; use them as your moments to learn.
2. Ask for help from the good people around you.
3. Keep balanced by working on things other than your sport.

You Say:

1. ....
....
2. ....
....
3. ....
....

I have seen too many young sports people with fantastic levels of talent who failed to make it because they didn't feel worthy. By completing this exercise as you have done, you are ensuring that this will not happen to you and that you will achieve the things you dream of. Think about it. Would you rather be a Matthew Pinsent or a Ben Johnson? I know which I would rather be!

Jonny Wilkinson won the world Cup for England with an awsome drop Kick, with just 35 seconds to go.

"... Jonny Wilkinson is Englands hero.."
He was given his debut by Sir Clive Woodward in 1998. (Thank you Sir Clive !!!.)

Chapter Eight

The Dreamer

'What a moment that was! We all worked so hard for it for so long, and it just proved that dreams, no matter how bold, really can come true'

Sir Clive Woodward, England Rugby coach

I was always being told off for daydreaming. Sometimes this was justified because I was just staring out of the window thinking about not very much at all and definitely not listening to what was going on in class.

Occasionally though, I was dreaming about the future, about what life would hold and where my place would be in it. I was dreaming of being great.

'All men dream but not equally, those who dream by night in the dusty recesses of their minds wake in the day to find that it was vanity; but the dreamers of the day are dangerous men, for they may act their dreams with open eyes, and make them real'

T. E. Lawrence (Lawrence of Arabia)

The Seven Pillars of Wisdom

Lawrence, coach and mentor to and motivator of the great Sir Winston Churchill, is telling us that we must dream, that great deeds are done only by those who dream of greatness in the first place.

Winston Churchill when only a young boy, said this to a friend at Harrow, who was so amazed by it that he wrote it down. He said that one day his country would be in great trouble and that he was destined to come to its rescue. Imagine carrying that around in your head. Churchill was dreaming of being great, like we all do.

What about you, do you dream of being great? I hope you do. I hope you spend time dreaming a great future for yourself, earned by working hard at something you have a talent for, something that you love.

Sometimes though, we lose sight of the future, we lose sight of all the great things we dreamed of. The drudgery of today gets in the way. The fact that we might be having a tough day starts us down a negative path and pretty soon the chemicals and dendrites are doing their thing and making us feel low.

We already have some techniques in place now to prevent this, don't we, but here is another!

I want you to play a game with me about the future. It is a game you will have played before, but not properly and not well enough.

I want you to write down a date which is ten years from now, to the day. Then I want you to fill the space by telling me about all the great things you have achieved. I don't want you to use words like 'I will', I want you to say things like 'last year I … ' or 'recently I have just … ', and 'at last we have finally managed to … '

In other words, I need you to imagine that you are writing to me on the date you write down and you are looking back on proud achievements that 'have happened'.

I first did this in 1996, when I was broke, had no idea what to do with my life, or where I wanted to go. The problem was that I was spending too much time looking back on all my failures instead of looking forward to all my successes, then I discovered that this was the way to do it. By the way, almost every single one of the unthinkable things I wrote down has happened! Amazing!

So, come on Dreamer, write me a letter now from the future, ten years from today.

Dear Mike,

Today is ……………………… and I am writing to you to let you know what I have achieved in the last few years. I am now….. years old and have had so much success in the last few years and I really wanted to tell you about it.

....

....

....

....

....

....

....

....

....

....

....

....

....

....

....

....

....

....

....

....

....

....

....

....

Remember Words-Pictures-Emotions? You have just written down words describing your future. The words should have generated powerful, happy pictures in your mind of you achieving the things you have written about. Then the chemicals (emotions) will be released, making you feel fantastic!

How good do you feel now? Look at what you have written. Look at the future you are creating for yourself. You are building dendrites which will form fully and then unleash your awesome talent and fulfil your destiny and your true potential.

It is impossible to think about these things in any depth unless you already have the potential to achieve them. Without that potential, they would simply not enter your mind. I never once dreamed of conducting an orchestra, or winning a Formula One race because, subconsciously, I know that the potential is not in me. There are, however, lots of things that I do dream of that are already taking shape in my mind.

Now, let's go again except, this time, imagine it is not ten but FIVE years from today.

Dear Mike,

Today is..................... and I am writing to let you know about all the great things I have been up to. I am now............ years old and life has been terrific!

....

....

....

....

....

....

....

....

....

....

....

....

....

....

....

....

....

....

....

....

....

....

They Did You Can

Okay, now can you see how the two exercises fit together? This should be taking shape nicely. The steps in your five-year plan are leading perfectly to your ten-year one.

Now, finally, let's go forward to a date just ONE year from today. Do the same again.

Dear Mike,

Today is.................... and it is one year since I read your book. I just wanted to let you know what I have done in that year and how proud I am of the changes and progress I have made.

You will be amazed how many of these great goals you will achieve, even only a year from now!

I now want you to do three things:

First   I want you to carry this with you and look at it often, because each time you do, you work on your dendrites, your destiny **(Intensity x Frequency or I x F)**.

Second I want you to do the whole exercise again once each year, so that you are constantly improving the detail of your future plans.

Third   I want you to summarise your ten-year dream into one statement. For example, I have put my own into a phrase which I now use as the welcome note on my mobile phone so that every time I switch my phone on, I am reminded of my mighty goals and purpose, of my reason to keep on going, no matter how tough it gets.

My Purpose

....

....

Your destiny is calling you! What are you waiting for?

I would have said the same to Karen Barber had I met her when she was sixteen. See if you can tell what I mean.

Karen represented Great Britain in two Olympic Games, in 1980 and 1984, was second in the British Championships six times in a row to Torville and Dean, won so many titles overseas she can't remember them all, was never out of the world's top ten for six years, and is now famous as Coach and Judge on *Dancing on Ice*.

Apart from all that, she is one of the most inspirational people you will ever meet.

'When I was fifteen, I was asked to go and see a Careers Teacher at school. I told her <u>I was going to be an Ice Skater</u>. She looked shocked. She asked me what my second choice was going to be. I didn't even understand the question. I told her I didn't need one; I was going to be an Ice Skater. The woman was obviously out of her depth; she just didn't understand. It was done; my choice was made.'

> **'I know where I'm going and I know the truth. I don't have to be what you want me to be. I'm free to be what I want'**
>
> Muhammad Ali

She was an averagely bright kid, seven **CSEs**, no trouble at school but not academic. She was a late developer. When she first stepped on the ice at six, there was no magic, no obvious special talent, she just loved it: *'I was a plodder.'* **Gordon Banks** says exactly the same about his football. *'I never thought I would compete at international level.'*

'The older kids used to have their own music playing on tapes as they practised but I didn't. They were at a much higher level than me but I used to imagine their music, their programme as we call it, was mine and I would dance to it as if it was. I never even got my own music until I was fourteen.'

Her progress though, between fourteen and sixteen, was like a whirlwind. How did she cope? *'I just went along with it. I trusted my coach and did as I was told'.*

Matthew Pinsent says that it was exactly the same for him in rowing – the coach was the boss, end of story. The coach told Pinsent what boat he would row in and he just rowed.

'One day, I got a new partner, Nicky Slater, whose Mum was my coach, and it just clicked, suddenly just clicked.'

Did she remember any low points early on? 'The only thing that I remember thinking could defeat me was that the other kids could afford so many lessons and I could only afford one each week, a twenty minute one. The rest of the week was spent practising what I had learned. During those twenty minutes, I listened to everything. Tuition didn't make me

"I achieved everything I wrote down on that plan, except that I was at the Olympics in 1980 AND 1984."

"If you fail to plan, you are planning to fail, So don't put it off, do it now!!!"

Karen Barber

what I was; remembering what the teacher had said and working on it all week did that.'

She remembers sitting in a school lesson one pivotal day. *'I made a plan spanning eight years. The plan included skating at national level and then I started thinking about the Olympics. I wrote down in big letters* **'Olympics 1984'***, then looked at it and thought, 'nah, I can do that before then,' so I crossed it out and put '1980'. I achieved everything I wrote down on that plan, except that I was at the Olympics in 1980 and 1984!'*

I wondered what her biggest strength was. *'I was just mentally strong. I never doubted myself. My biggest strength was me, it wasn't coaching; I didn't have enough coaching in a week, remember. I do also have a really good memory for steps, I used to write them all down and draw patterns; I was just very motivated.'*

Was that only around ice skating? *'No, I was like that with everything. I was and I am. I wanted to succeed. I outgrew people in my class, had less and less in common. I was up at four thirty in the morning five days a week by then. I was just an average kid, but I could hold my own at most things and could have made another career in PR or something using what I now know are my people skills. I was never going to be a brain surgeon though.*

I made tremendous sacrifices, just like my Mum and Dad had done, so I was always going to make it work. I lived in a bedsit for four years with very little money, counting it to the penny. I moved from the north down to Richmond and I got by on whatever I could.'

Yet, by her own admission, she was no shining star in terms of her talent. *'Talent? What I know now is that talented kids can be quite lazy; whereas motivated kids with a bit of talent are the ones you want. I was one of those. Those without talent don't have it easy and they are the best kind of people. As a coach, you'd rather have the child with the motivation and a bit of talent because you know they will work so hard. I remember one kid, with no finances at all, who is now skating at junior world level and just starting her first professional skating job in Portugal.'*

How did she get through to her? *'I just talked to her, encouraged her, let her feel I believed in her. I have one skater who was registered with special needs at school but has completely turned around, winning national events, achieving every goal I have set him. He is no longer on the special needs register. This kid had seen social workers, had family problems like alcoholism, you name it. But get them to enjoy something, anything, get them to start winning, believe in them. If you do, they will.*

*I suppose the ultimate proof of that is this Dancing on Ice thing; the celebrities want to learn so do, and very quickly, but not because of talent, because they want to. And Mike, you taught me to look for attitude in people by asking them how they are and listening to the response. I love it now when I ask a kid how they are. One might say, "I'm a bit tired" and I know that it isn't going to happen today for that kid, but listen to another one say, "yeah, great", and I think "that's the right kind of character". I say to my girls, "**if you fail to plan, you are planning to fail**, so don't put it off, do it now!" Give me any kid who wants to learn, make them believe they can do it, and they will. Even kids who aren't going to skate for a living will get motivated through applying themselves to their skating or whatever. What I always ask them to do is, "just be the best you can be". That's all people will ever ask of you, isn't it, just be the best you can be.*

You get to your teenage years and it is so easy to just go off the rails, you know, it can be hard to talk to people but, if you can manage your time, just make a little bit of time for everything, you can get through, you really can. I only believe in positive, I don't do the other side, the negative, I just don't do it.'

Coach Says

1. Make a plan for your future achievements.
2. Do it now!
3. Just be the best you can be.

You Say:

1. ....
....

2. ....
....

3. ....
....

Have you written down your goals and dreams above? Somebody once told me that you'll never see statues of critics, you will only ever see statues of people who dreamed and achieved great things. I want to be one of those and I hope you do too.

'Come on! Go for it.'

Chapter Nine

Go Get It

Well, there you are then, you now know what I know about setting and achieving goals to fulfil your destiny and potential, and containing the secrets of success, peace of mind, happiness and what my old mate Indy called '**Fortune and Glory**'

Eleanor Roosevelt said that:

'The future belongs to those who believe in the beauty of their dreams'

And now you know that she was right.

You have learned the secrets to the mental mastery of all performance situations, which you can apply not only to your sport but to your life, whether you need help with exams at school, learning to drive, coping with the pressure of a health issue, leaping out of a plane or whatever it is that life throws at you.

You now have the power and you know that you always did, we just forgot to tell you!

Look at the challenges we face in life:

Confidence

Others say: *'I want it, but don't think I am good enough.'*

You say: *'Of course I am good enough, and I will prove it!'*

Ha! Beaten that one!

Focus

Others say: *'I just don't have any goals or direction. I don't know what I am good at or what I want to do'.*

You say: *'I know exactly what I want and am moving relentlessly towards it. I know my purpose and my goals, for the long and short term, in all areas of my life.'*

There! Another one bites the dust!

Loneliness

Others say: *'Nobody believes in me, nobody takes me seriously, I have no support.'*

You say: *'Supporters are welcome and those who do not believe or care are welcome too, because they drive me on (Look at Robbie Williams' poem 'Hello Sir, Remember Me' in Chapter 12 and how he made, it in spite of the negativity), so I thank them all!'*

Right! Next.

Failure

Come on! Go for it.

This is getting boring now isn't it?

You see, what 'the others' do not know and what we do know, is that ***'Life is only ten percent about the Facts, and ninety percent about the Mind.'***

Success lies in conquering the use of the power of the mind which is exactly what you have now learned to do. All you need to do now is go out and practise.

You have techniques to help you out in the short term, the long term, when things go well and when things go badly. You have learned the skill of **visualisation**, **concentration**, **relaxation**, **determination** and any other **'ation'** you can name.

Combine what you have learned with the skills you already possess and the power you were born with; the combination is potent and powerful beyond measure.

Did you see the film, *Coach Carter* starring Samuel L. Jackson as the College Basketball Coach? It's a great film to illustrate what we have been looking at, but there is one kid in his team, Timo Cruz, who Jackson 'picks' on.

This kid is sulky so one day Jackson shouts at him across the gym,

"What is your deepest fear?"

All the other kids on the team wonder what Jackson is talking about and why he keeps on asking this one kid this one question,

"What is your deepest fear?"

Then, towards the end of the film, Jackson asks him the question again and turns to walk away. Timo stands up and, in front of the whole team, answers Coach Carter's question, and here is a beautiful part of what he says:

"We ask ourselves, *Who am I to be brilliant, gorgeous, handsome, talented and fabulous?*"

(This is a quote from some famous words written by a brilliant lady called Marianne Williamson, founder of the Peace Alliance, which Nelson Mandela IS OFTEN SAID TO HAVE used in his inaugural speech. Google the sentence and you can see the rest of what she says.

Coach Carter smiles and knows that Cruz now realises that the sulks were not caused by his failures. His sulks were caused by his unwillingness to face up to the fact that he was talented and that success was not something he was used to.

Coach Carter knew that Timo and the team had learned to live with, to celebrate and to enjoy their talent, to welcome the attention and the limelight that comes with success, to bathe in the joy of success, rather than run away from it, like most people do.

We all have within us the power to achieve something great.

The only person who can stop me is me; the only person who could have stopped you was you. Now this has all changed. You know this and how to achieve whatever it is in life that you set your mind to.

Get out there! Make it happen. What are you waiting for? Go Get It!

Chapter Ten

Secrets of Great Teams and Individuals

> **'Never doubt that a small group of committed individuals can change the world; in fact it is all that ever has'**
>
> Sir Winston Churchill

The Australian Cricket Team is probably the greatest EVER. What is it that makes it so great?

1. They are incredibly talented. They probably have as many 'all time great player' contenders as any team has ever had.

2. They appear to feel ferociously proud, passionate and privileged to play for their team; humble and grateful for the opportunity they have been given.

3. They appear determined to want to be remembered for being truly great.

4. They contest every single moment of every single day with 'most important moment ever' mentality; they give their very best when it counts.

5. They appear to believe one hundred percent in their ability to do what is needed now.

6. They appear desperate to win every ball, every session, every day, every game and every series.

7. Constantly they appear alert, fresh, excited and enthusiastic, as if it is the first day, game or big occasion of their careers.

8. They respond appropriately and competitively to niggles from the opposition; they can handle themselves in a conflict situation.

9. Their confidence is not 'bravado', it is a mature, unconscious representation of who they perceive themselves to be; they just honestly believe that they are the best and embrace that, revel in it, enjoy it, welcome it, thrive on it.

10. They are incredibly fit and strong, surely as a result of hard work off the field.

11. They know what they are supposed to be doing and they do it, remaining clear-thinking and calm at all times.

12. Individuals are supported through failure within the team's game plan without being criticised or omitted. They become part of a stable unit, not always playing, but always involved.

There appear to be TWELVE ingredients essential for success:

1. Talented
2. Dutiful
3. Ambitious
4. Competitive
5. Unwavering
6. Focused
7. Enthusiastic
8. Tough
9. Mature
10. Fit
11. Methodical
12. Secure

TWO are physical qualities, the other TEN are mental

ALL TWELVE CAN BE LEARNED

ALL TWELVE APPLY TO ANY INDIVIDUAL OR TEAM

How many on our list apply to:

Individual

Tiger Woods (¹²⁄₁₂)

Tiger always has a plan and sticks to it and is very comfortable in his skin. He undoubtedly wants to become the greatest golfer of all time, obviously works very hard at his game and appears to be a thoroughly decent bloke.

Muhammad Ali (¹²⁄₁₂)

Ali always believed in himself and wanted to be the best. He was a pioneer in sport, very different from anything that had gone before and he lived in troubled times, relying heavily on support from his close family. In later life Ali has shown his true value.

Roger Federer (¹²⁄₁₂)

Relentless in pursuit of greatness, always modest and respectful, Federer, like Woods, seems determined to achieve greatness. He is even-tempered although he is surrounded by 'hype' with which he copes easily.

Listen to this, by Jonathan Davies, possibly the greatest outside half in the entire history of Welsh Rugby, and just imagine a team full of people who think like this.

'When I was playing rugby at school my PE Teacher Meirion Davies in-stilled a work ethic in us all. Teamwork and team spirit was essential but more importantly, in an enjoyable way, discipline – without us even realis-ing it! I always used what I learnt with Meirion in the way I trained and played rugby.

As I got older and more 'serious' about the sport I always took pride in my performance, not wanting to let the team or myself down. There

The perfectly timed pass, the pace, the assured boot
and the eye for the gap, that exciting commentary!
Rugby legend Jonathan Davies.

was a 'fear of failure' in me, which I controlled, and this drove me on to succeed.

From a young age I was in awe of the talent of the rugby players I saw on the television or read about in the press. I soon realised that I too could be good enough to play against or with them. I set my goal to be as good as and better than them, and was soon on the rugby pitch with them!

It does not matter where you live, what your family background is or how talented you are academically. Never say

'**IF** only I had done ...'
'**IF** only I had the opportunity ...'
'**IF** only I had been in the right place ...'
'**IF** only ...'

IF is a BIG word, but **IF you** *believe in your ability, like all of the sporting heroes in this book, take up the challenge* **YOU** *can make a difference!*

Team

The England Rugby Team World Cup 2003 $\left(\frac{12}{12}\right)$

Comfortable being built up as favourites for the tournament, they were solid as a team, hated to be beaten and always found a way to win even when not playing fluently. The players respected and totally trusted each other.

Manchester United 1999 Treble $\left(\frac{12}{12}\right)$

This team performed under intense physical pressure to win three major trophies in one season in the face of incredible competition and against overwhelming odds, where the sheer number of games meant that this feat had never been achieved by any team before.

England Cricket Team 2005 Ashes ⑫/12

Every player performed to their limit and never lost confidence, even after going 1-0 down to the best team of all time. Players showed a lot of control and focus to withstand the fight against truly great players.

You could try and pick one quality at a time and work on it to make yourself the best you can be and build your own confidence in your abilities.

Go on, try it!

Chapter Eleven

What it Takes to Succeed at Anything

Twelve Quick Tips

1. Ask

Find yourself a person you can talk to. Make it a person you respect. Make it a person who thinks a lot of you too. Make it a person who can help you with good advice. Make it a person you can be open with. Tell them honestly how you are feeling and what help you need. If you trust them, listen to them. Remember how that helped Jeremy Snape?

2. Dream

Spend as much time as you can, thinking about what it is going to be like when you really have arrived at the place you want to go. What does it feel like? What are people saying to you? What are you saying to them? What advice are you giving to people who want to achieve what you have achieved? Amanda Kirby calls this 'visualising' and asks her gymnasts to do it often. Karen Barber imagined competing at the Olympics, Mary Peters dreamed of Gold and Philip Neville focused on driving away in his brand new Honda Prelude! Dreaming works but only if you are prepared to dream 'long enough and hard enough' (as Johnny Depp says to Dustin Hoffman in *Finding Neverland*).

3. Focus

Be very specific about your goals. I never was. I wanted to 'play for Blackburn Rovers'. I wanted to 'pull on the number 9 shirt'. I did these things but I only played in the Reserve and Youth teams. In reality, I did achieve my goals but they were the WRONG goals. Be more specific about your goals. Remember Mary's story about that nail? When Mary asked Mary Rand and Ann Packer what they were doing, when she saw them knocking nails into the wall, they didn't say 'knocking these nails into the wall to hang our medals on'; they said 'knocking these nails into the wall to hang our gold medals on'. That's different. It was the difference between gold or silver and bronze. Be clear about what you want. Precise. Exact.

A word of warning though, 'Be careful what you wish for, you are likely to get it' – which means, don't wish harm to others to achieve your aims; get there on your own merits.

4. Reflect

Keep a special book in which you can write the lessons you have learned. I once met a guy who was a rugby player and went to Durham University when Rory Underwood was there. The rugby players tended to live together in houses and these houses became known as 'rugby houses' and a bit of a status symbol, a sign that you 'were somebody'.

Anyway, this guy moves into one of these rugby houses in his second year and starts to unpack in his room. He opens a drawer and finds a book inside, like a big diary. He realises that it is a rugby diary, containing details of every single first team game of the previous season. It lists the date, the opposition, the conditions, the score and a match report; impressive, but not especially interesting. But then he sees what's written at the bottom of each page under two headings. The first is 'What I learned today', beneath which the writer recorded what he learned as a player. The second is one he thought was a bit weird. It said 'What I learned today for when I am England Captain'. The guy could hardly believe it. The formula was repeated for every match. He read them all.

It was obvious that this book was lost and he just knew that he had to return it, which he did, to a very grateful man indeed.

That guy was Will Carling. He did become Captain of England and led his team to many great successes with great distinction.

5. Affirm

Write down specific goals and read them every day, before you set out in the morning and before you go to sleep at night. These goals should be for the short and long term, and for all the important parts of your life. Karen Barber's goal was written when she was only sixteen but it came true. Ah, the power of the dendrite!

6. Think

Remember, your confidence and focus are never more than ONE thought away. Make every single thought a positive one and, if you do have a negative one, aggressively reject it and turn it around. (You might want to do this quietly, so as not to scare anyone!) Gordon Banks talked about 'pushing' the negative out of your mind. You have the power to choose your thoughts, always, so choose positive ones!

7. Promise

Learn from Mary Peters and find your equivalent of putting your nail in the wall. You do not have to do this right now but do it when you are ready. Make your promise to yourself, make a visual reminder of it, and keep it.

8. Work

Stay one step ahead. Remember what Phil said about Sir Alex Ferguson; work harder than anyone else and it will give you peace of mind, knowing that you are in the best shape you can possibly be in.

9. Remember

If it ever gets too hard or too much, remember WHY you are doing it. Stop and remind yourself what you want and how great that is. Then ask yourself if it is worth it. You will find that the answer is that what Phil Neville calls 'sacrifice' is worth it and that feeling low, as Jeremy found out when he literally sat in that gutter, is part of feeling high. Only by feeling low will you know how much winning really means to you.

10. Learn

Read Michel Jordan's book *I Can't Accept Not Trying* and other books by your heroes. You'll find out they were just like you, not always the perfect heroes you imagine them to be. You will find out that they too had times when they felt low. Karen talked about her intelligence helping her get the most out of her precious skating lessons, so even those of us who are not academic need to work on our learning skills to help us with our sport. Remember also how learning spectacularly turned around Doctor Ben Carson's life!

11. Fail

When you fail, take the lessons, not the guilt. You will face defeat at some point, so learn from it. There is no shame in defeat; there is only shame in not bouncing back, even when you feel 'like a dog' as Gary Kirsten taught us!

That which does not kill us makes us stronger

12. Identify

Get a motto with which you can identify, which sums up you and your approach. Everton's is 'Nil satis nisi optimum', which means 'only the best will do'; Bolton Wanderers' is 'Supera Moras', meaning 'overcome all obstacles' which they hadn't used since the 1950s until we resurrected it for them. Our family motto is 'Never Give In'. What's yours? It doesn't have to be in Latin!

This was Will Carling's, written by US President Roosevelt. Back in 2000, we did some work with Will through some mutual friends and, not long after, he was being interviewed on BBC Radio and the presenter asked him if he valued any particular speech or quotation. Carling, who was a great Captain, chose these. I think they are awesome words, telling us to hold up our heads whenever we compete and to give our best.

The Man In The Arena

It is not the critic who counts; not the man who points out how the strong man stumbles, or where the doer of deeds could have done them better.

The credit belongs to the man who is actually in the arena, whose face is marred by dust and sweat and blood; who strives valiantly; who errs, who comes short again and again, because there is no effort without error and shortcoming; but who does actually strive to do the deeds; who knows great enthusiasms, the great devotions; who spends himself in a worthy cause; who at the best knows in the end the triumph of high achievement and who, at the worst if he fails, at least fails while daring greatly, so that his place shall never be with those cold and timid souls who neither know victory nor defeat.

Chapter Twelve

A Message for The Coach, Teacher, Mentor or Parent

Remember Chapter 2, The Best Friend? Well you may want to give this chapter to your 'coach', the person who's supporting you and keeping you on track. This will help them to understand what it is you are going through and what kind of encouragement you will need.

Tips for The Coach From The Top

This whole book is about young people needing to be encouraged. They won't thrive on being humiliated or pulled up constantly for their failings. They have to be given the support and courage to achieve what that can become. My experience in professional sport is that, when people feel low, they cannot handle criticism. They can only deal with it when they feel good about themselves, so this is where you play such an important role. Obviously there will be a need for criticism but it has to come from a basis of trust. If not, the young person will only feel disliked and they will not take on board what you have to say.

Take a leaf out of Muhammad Ali's story about his mother who told him that his confidence in himself made her believe in him. In fact, he said it was the other way around as it was her confidence in him that strengthened his belief in himself. Ben Carson had the same story too.

Here are some tips from people who have been coached by the best and have made it to the top of their mountain, so probably have some insights that are of value.

Gary Kirsten

Create an atmosphere of trust so that your players can 'unpack their vulnerability'.

Tell them about when you struggled and don't go on about all your successes or how great YOU were. Be humble. Relate to people in terms of where they are on their tough journey.

Karen Barber

Encourage and instil confidence. Believe in them and you will get them to believe they are good.

Ensure they develop wider interests to sharpen their minds so that they can coach with the intellectual challenge of personal growth.

Gordon Banks

Make sure they are enjoying practise and loving what they do.

Jeremy Snape

Make sure they are surrounded by good people, with good values.

Amanda Kirby

Always end a critique on a positive and always tell them what you want, not what you don't want. Can you imagine going up to a counter in an ice cream shop and, when the person says 'Hello, what can I get you?' you say 'Well, not Vanilla!' We would never do that, we would say 'Chocolate Please!' but we will say to people 'Don't miss!' or 'Don't let me down!' rather than 'Hit the target!' or 'Make me proud!' The message is clear, give positive instructions!

> *'Keep your mind on the things you want and off the things you don't want'*
>
> Art Niemann

You have to be able to relate to people; use words they understand, not big words.

Push them harder to test their ambition.

Let them see you watching them and noticing them; praise them when they get it right, and coach them by offering a positive tip when they do not.

Beth Tweddle

Make them visualise, especially when they cannot train.

Philip Neville

Be the example to them in terms of your work rate; they will probably not work harder than you do, so set the pace.

Now, take another look at my list of 'What it Takes to Succeed at Anything' from the previous chapter.

A Checklist for the Coach

It is a list of twelve qualities, two physical and ten mental.

These qualities can be taught and learned but, as Coach, you must be able to spot that these are or are not present, then take action to support the individual or the team.

This checklist can be used by you or by them, both individually and in terms of how it applies to the team.

I often hear coaches talk about readiness for competition using the words, Technical, Tactical, Physical and Mental; in other words, checking that they are prepared in these four key areas. My checklist simply amplifies that and demands that we assess it in more detail.

Most of the items on this list relate to the state of mind of the individual or collective state of mind of the unit. Correction of these takes time, care and expertise.

The mental list relates to the self image and self esteem of the person or the unit. You will sense an element of clinical ruthlessness in the truly great, which is often perceived as arrogance, but this often masks the life of a person who draws strength from a solid set of values and principles, given to them either by parents or guardians, coaches or teachers.

This role is one that you, as Coach, need to ensure is present in the life of your athletes, and may well even be one which you have to fulfil for them yourself; remember the Karate Kid and Mister Miyoge? Think of Samuel L. Jackson in *Coach Carter*.

For 'Coach', substitute the words 'Teacher', 'Mentor' and even 'Parent' to give a clearer picture of exactly what it is that the athlete might need from you.

A person or team lacking self respect, or self esteem, will under-achieve on potential, no matter how well prepared Technically, Physically or Tactically, so ignore this 'softer' side of coaching at your peril.

Digest the wisdom in this concluding quote from a 1999 magazine article on Tiger:

'What will be my abiding impression of this young man? Simply that he is disconcertingly comfortable with his own brilliance. I am so glad that I am a journalist and not a golfer'

Time Magazine

Question	Yes/No Focus On:
1. Talented Is s/he or are we really good enough to achieve?	
2. Dutiful Does s/he or do we show respect for ourselves, the opportunity, the opponent?	
3. Ambitious Does s/he or do we have aggressive long-term goals?	
4. Competitive Does s/he or do we fight for every little thing?	
5. Unwavering Does s/he or do we show that we believe when it counts?	
6. Focused Can s/he or can we show sustained concentration for long enough periods?	

Question	Yes/No Focus On:

7. Enthusiastic

Does s/he or do we bounce into every practice session and competition?

8. Tough

Can s/he or can we look after ourselves in battle?

9. Mature

Is s/he or are we accepting of our talent?

10. Fit

Is s/he or are we really as fit as we need to be?

11. Methodical

Does s/he or do we ruthlessly carry out plans?

12. Secure

Does s/he or do we feel accepted?

SUMMARY

....

....

....

....

....

Mr. Robert Williams.

Robbie Williams inspired me to come up with a message to all coaches. I suppose, to really understand my point here, you will need to listen to Robbie's poem at the end of his sensational album, *Life Through A Lens*. My alternative based on his is a contrast to the teacher who called him 'thingy' and didn't want him to fly. When it comes to our time, maybe it would be nice if the people we try to help and encourage wrote something a little more like this.

Fortune and Glory

Hello Sir, remember me?
I'm the Star you knew I'd always be,
The child from whom you removed all fears
You called me 'Genius' for six whole years.
Yeh, that's right, I could be Bob,
The one who landed the Pop Star's job,
The kid you said had The Golden Touch
The kid you said would achieve so much.
And so I'm here, and you're still there
With your cool sports car and receding hair
Same silly trousers that you thought were smart
Married to the woman who stole your heart
Devoted to our lives, devoted to the school
'I wanna be a Star, Sir', you thought that was cool!
'Be a Star, that's not so barmy,
Make that your goal and forget the Army'
And you worked so hard to tell us this,
That the dreams we had we would not miss.
Sir is God, he's decided it's right
To help build our dreams with all his might.
So thanks for the advice, I'm sure it will do
For every kid I ever knew.
You really were right – I'm a Mega Civilian
I don't lead my life riding pillion
You turned me into a focused weapon
'Fortune and Glory' are about to beckon
And here I sit, Sir, in First Class
Thanks to you, I'll kick Life's Ass.

Thanks Robbie for the inspiration!

Michael Finnigan

And Finally ...

You are going to have tremendous successes as a result of applying the techniques you have learned in this book and I want to hear all about them, so please be sure to let me know.

Of course you may, at some point, find you need a little extra support or encouragement, either for yourself or for a person you are attempting to help and, if that happens, I want you to ask me if I have any advice.

In either case, contact me by e-mail at:

mike@theydidyoucan.co.uk

I promise you a personal, private and confidential response in double quick time.

Alternatively, you may want more information about all the great things our business does to help people and organisations all over the world be the very best they can possibly be as they pursue their goals and dreams and strive to fulfil their potential.

If so, look up our details on the worldwide web at:

www.theydidyoucan.co.uk

My success is your success, so please do not hesitate to get in touch.

Come On!

Bibliography

A Golden Age   Steve Redgrave
(BBC Worldwide Ltd 2000)

A Return to Love   Marianne Williamson
(Harper Collins 1992)
Contains the quote we all know

Behind the White Ball
                    Jimmy White with Rosemary Kingsland
(Hutchinson 1998)
I'm in this one! Our first sports client tells his story

Blink   Malcolm Gladwell
(Penguin 2006)

Learn to trust your instincts! Mind blowing examples about the speed of decisions!

Every Second Counts
                    Lance Armstrong with Sally Jenkins
(Yellow Jersey 2003)
Better than the first book for me, and what a story!

155

Flow. The Classic Work on How to Achieve Happiness
Mihaly Csikszentmihalyi

(Harper & Row 2002)

Classic academic text, heavy but brilliant

Gifted Hands   Ben Carson

(Zondervan 1996)

An amazing story of the world's most famous doctor

Gordon Banks: A Hero who Could Fly   Don Mullan

(A little book company 2006)

A compelling story about the power we can unknowingly exert over the lives of others by a friend of mine and a fantastic human being. Foreword by actor Gabriel Byrne

Greatest Business Stories of all Time   Daniel Gross

(John Wiley & Sons Inc 1996)

Greg Norman   Lauren St John

(Bantam 1998)

Live through the ups and downs with this great optimist and world number one golfer

How to Win Friends and Influence People   Dale Carnegie

(Simon & Schuster 1936)

This man was a genius in the field of human relationships

Human Instinct   Professor Robert Winston

(Bantam Press 2002)

We all know this guy, and this book is a joy!

I Can't Accept Not Trying   Michael Jordan
(Harper Collins 2004)

A truly inspirational short book on the pursuit of excellence

Jack. What I've Learned Leading a Great Company and Great People   Jack Welch
(Warner Books Inc 2001)

King of the World   David Remnick
(Random House 1999)

Detailed insights into Ali's boxing life and times

Managing My Life   Sir Alex Ferguson
(Hodder and Stoughton 1999)

Get inside the mind of a great leader, and a true warrior

Man's Search for Meaning   Victor Frankl
(Hodder & Stoughton 1964)

Harrowing read, but another classic work on the power of the human mind

Mary P   Mary Peters with Ian Woolridge
(Stanley Paul 1974)

Mary's story is almost unbelievable, especially her account of winning her gold medal

Message of a Master   John MacDonald
(New World Library 1993)

My all time favourite. Breath-taking, timeless wisdom and THE secret of the ancients

They Did You Can

Muhammad Ali Through the Eyes of the World
Compiled by Mark Collings

(MPG Books 2001)

How world figures see 'The Greatest' is fantastic to hear. Will something like this be written about us one day? I hope so

Never Give In   Winston S Churchill

(Pimlico 2004)

This guy was a fearless leader and an inspirational speaker

Peak Performance   Gilson, Pratt, Wymes, Roberts

(Profile Books 2003)

A brilliant insight from my friends Clive, Mike and Kevin into the world's greatest sporting organisations

Personal Best   Denise Lewis

(Century 2001)

Psycho-Cybernetics   Maxwell Maltz

(Wilshire Books 1999)

Maltz was a plastic surgeon. This book about self esteem is magnificent

Raising the Bar: The Championship Years
of Tiger Woods   Tim Rosaforte

(St Martin's Press 2000)

Great stories which tell you a lot about Tiger's amazing mental strength

Seize the Day   Tanni Grey Thompson
(Hodder 2001)

Tires you out just reading it! Not one ounce of self pity in here

Serious   John McEnroe with James Kaplan
(Little, Brown 2002)

A winner, a genius, a straight talker

Somebody Someday   Robbie Williams
(Ebury 2001)

*The story of a man with so much talent who is fighting so many demons.
Come on Robbie!*

The Complete Works   William Shakespeare
(Magpie 1993)

Full of fantastic quotes for you to mull over

The Collected Clinical Works   Alfred Adler
(Adler Institute 1999)

Adler's view on how to help people is selfless, refreshing and timeless

The Diving Bell and the Butterfly
                 Jean Dominique Bauby
(Knopf 1997)

Saddest book I have ever read, but truly inspirational if you can take it

The First Four Minutes   Roger Bannister
(Puttnam 1955)

Still one of the greatest moments not only in sport but in history

They Did You Can

The Greatest Miracle in the World   Og Mandino

(Frederick Fell Publishers 1994)

The Luck Factor   Richard Wiseman

(Arrow 2003)

Fascinating study into luck, you'll love it and learn how to use it

The Man who Listens to Horses   Monty Roberts

(Roberts 2002)

My friend Monty has a terrific story to tell you. Forget the horse angle, this is about life!

The Nation's Favourite Poems

       Foreword by Griff Rhys Jones

(BBC Books 1996)

100 poems, some of which you will love and be inspired by, especially 'If' by Kipling

The Penguin Book of 20th Century Speeches

       Brian MacArthur

(Penguin 1999)

Filled with brilliant ideas and eloquent words

The Private Life of the Brain   Susan Greenfield

(Penguin 2001)

She makes the complex appear simple. Awesome stuff!

The Richest Man in Babylon   George S. Clason

(New American Library 1988)

The Soul of a Butterfly   Muhammad Ali
(Bantam 2005)

Where does this man's talent end? Proves he is more than a big-headed boxer!

The Success System that Never Fails   W. Clement Stone
(Pocket Books 1980)

Stone is THE man. He was mentor to one of my mentors and this is a classic

The Tao of Muhammad Ali   Davis Miller
(Vintage 1997)

A normal person like you and me meets Ali and becomes his friend

The Tipping Point   Malcolm Gladwell
(Abacus 2001)

The Winner Within   Pat Riley
(Riles & Company Inc 1994)

The Wisdom of Crowds   James Surowiecki
(Abacus 2004)

I found this stunning. Some of the examples of statistics will amaze you and change the way you decide things

Think and Grow Rich   Napoleon Hill
(Ross Cornwell 2004)

First published in 1937, this is the first and for many years was the only book on the positive power of your mind. It is superbly written

They Did You Can

Touching the Void   Joe Simpson
(Vintage 1997)

Waiting for the Mountain to Move   Charles Handy
(Jossey-Bass 1995)

Anything by Handy is a must. He is one of the leading thinkers of all time and inspirational to read

Winning   Sir Clive Woodward
(Hodder & Stoughton 2004)

Sir Clive has written a great piece for this book, and his own is a definitive and comprehensive guide for any team wanting to learn how to win

Index

Praise for They Did You Can

Being a young sport loving person I enjoyed this book a lot and would recommend it to anyone who like me lives a life of sport and dreams of getting to the top one day. It gives an insight into what the pro's and the legends did to get where they are and what hurdles you will come up against in the journey to the top.

They Did You Can, is an inspiration for young people who dream about being like their heroes. Anyone who wants to be world champion or to stand alongside their heroes should really read this book to find out what it takes to get there.

It's a brilliant way to find out how the stars got to where they are and what attitude you need to be the best. For young people who love their sport whether it be Football, Rugby, Athletics or anything else this book is the perfect word in the ear you need to succeed!

If you want to stand on the podium at the Olympics one day or run out in the world cup final for your country then TDYC is the perfect read for you and may even help you get there and lift that trophy or wear that winner's medal!

Alex Lambert — Age 16

The great thing about this book is that it will help you whatever your level of interest. If you put into action the ideas in this book, you will find that 'winning' is well within your reach.

Sir Clive Woodward – England Rugby Union World Cup winning coach, Director of Elite Performance British Olympic Association

Mike Finnigan is to be congratulated for what he has achieved with this book. Through some of the great sportsmen and women of our lifetime, he introduces us to ordinary people who, through dedication and hard work, have lived extraordinary lives. This book is about encouragement.

Don Mullan — author of *Gordon Banks – a Hero who could fly*